PUFFIN BOOKS
LET'S GO TIME TRAVELLING

Subhadra Sen Gupta has written over twenty-five books for children, including mysteries, historical adventures, ghost stories and comic books. Right now she is waiting for someone to build a time machine so that she can travel to the past and join Emperor Akbar for lunch.

She loves to travel, flirt with cats, chat with auto-rickshaw drivers and sit and watch people.

GW00578017

Read Other Books in Puffin by Subhadra Sen Gupta

Let's Go Time Travelling!

LIFE IN INDIA THROUGH THE AGES

SUBHADRA SEN GUPTA

Illustrated by Tapas Guha

PUFFIN BOOKS

An imprint of Penguin Random House

PUFFIN BOOKS

USA | Canada | UK | Ireland | Australia
New Zealand | India | South Africa | China

Puffin Books is part of the Penguin Random House group of companies
whose addresses can be found at global.penguinrandomhouse.com

Published by Penguin Random House India Pvt. Ltd
4th Floor, Capital Tower 1, MG Road,
Gurugram 122 002, Haryana, India

Penguin
Random House
India

First published in Puffin by Penguin Books India 2012

10 9 8 7 6 5 4 3 2

ISBN 9780143331919

Typeset in Archer by Eleven Arts, Keshav Puram, New Delhi

Printed at Repro India Limited

www.penguin.co.in

MIX
Paper from
responsible sources
FSC® C047271

CONTENTS

INTRODUCTION

What is This Book All About

One: EARLY INDIA

Two: ANCIENT INDIA

Three: MEDIEVAL INDIA

Four: BRITISH INDIA

MORE HISTORY HUNGAMA

WHAT IS THIS BOOK ALL ABOUT?

WHAT IS THIS BOOK ALL ABOUT?

This book is about history true, but you can be sure of one thing.
It is not about kings, battles and dates. And you won't have to
take a test on it. It talks of all the colourful and human things
that are interesting about history.

It is about how people lived in the past. So you'll discover what
they ate for lunch in Harappa (crocodile curry) and whether
women in Mauryan India put on make-up (yes, they did). Did
children go to school (some did), did their gurus give them
homework (of course not!). Everything from houses, fashion,
food, sports, board games, theatre, elephants and palanquins;
all the weird, freaky stuff that you never find in textbooks finds
mention here. So I'm hoping you'll have fun.

So okay, I read a lot of fat books and dug out all the information,
but this book wouldn't have happened without three very
important people. There is of course my friend Tapas Guha,
who went crazy drawing all the funny cartoons, and also my
two fabulous editors, Sudeshna Shome Ghosh and Sohini Mitra,

who made some really clever suggestions. The idea of having a story in the beginning of each chapter is their brainwave. Finally if you have any questions, ideas of what you want me to write next or even rude comments, mail me at subhadrasg@gmail.com. I promise to reply.

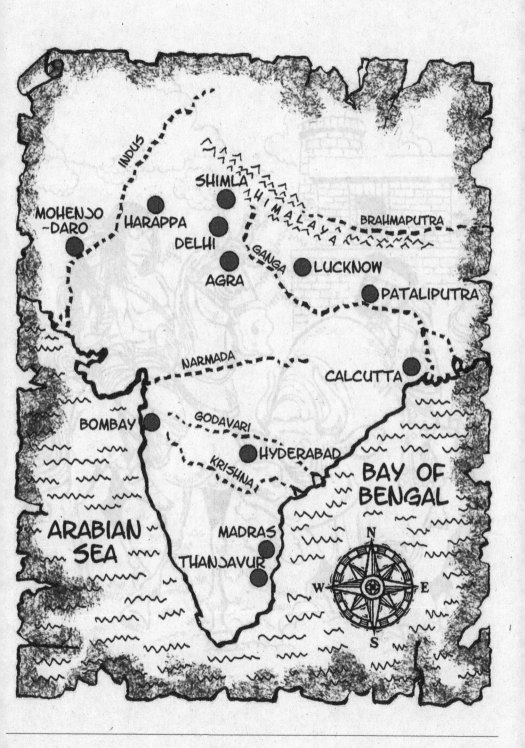

One: EARLY INDIA

The Harappan Civilization
The Indo-Aryans

THE HARAPPAN CIVILIZATION
(2600 BCE–1500 BCE)

A DAY IN THE LIFE OF URPI

Urpi and her older brother, Kira, accompanied their father to the market. There they laid out the earthen bowls and pans that he had made on his potter's wheel. Nearby, a woman sat with a pile of fresh vegetables; the fisherman had laid out rows of fish that he had caught in the river that morning; and a farmer had parked his bullock cart in the corner, piled high with baskets of grain.

The workers from the granary were carrying baskets to the warehouse at the top of the Citadel where the grain was stored. So whenever their mother needed wheat or barley, she would go to the granary to buy some. Just then a woman came to buy two bowls and paid for them with a bunch of bananas. That made Kira smile as he loved bananas. Urpi wished someone would pay for the pottery with a few beads, for the new necklace that she was stringing together.

Urpi watched an important man walk past—it was the High Priest from the Citadel temple, wearing his flowered dress, a diadem around his forehead and a stone seal hung around his chest. They both stood up and bowed to him, but he was too busy to notice the two children standing behind their stall of pottery.

'The High Priest goes past every day and we always bow, but he never smiles at us,' said Kira, puzzled.

'Why should he—we are just the children of a potter. If our father had been a rich trader sending ships to the west he would smile at us,' Urpi said shortly.

'Then we should ask Father to become a trader and send our pottery to the city of Ur. That would please the High Priest, won't it?'

'Hah!' Urpi swung her pigtails. 'I can make him smile any day I want. Just watch me.'

'You do that and I will get you more beads.'

'How? Like magic?' asked Urpi disdainfully.

'I am growing carrots at the back of the house. I'll exchange a basket of them for beads.'

'Done! High Priest here I come!' declared Urpi.

The children knew that in the afternoon the High Priest headed home for lunch. As he came down the steps of the temple, Urpi ran up to him carrying a pretty pottery bowl and bowing said, 'A gift for Your Honour.'

'Oh!' the High Priest stopped in surprise. 'What a beautiful bowl and it is a gift for me?'

'I admire you, sir. You are such a great and powerful priest.'

As the High Priest took the bowl from Urpi he gave a wide, toothy smile, 'Thank you my child!' and still smiling, walked away.

Urpi skipped back to their stall in triumph, 'See! Everyone likes a free gift, even our gloomy High Priest!'

'True! And flattery makes everyone smile,' sighed Kira. 'I'll start picking the carrots.'

◆ ◆ ◆

Urpi and Kira lived at Mohenjo-daro, and what is amazing is that we know quite a lot about how they lived, even though it was nearly five thousand years ago.

It all began with huge piles of muddy brown bricks and broken walls that could be seen in the desert lands of Sind and Western Punjab in today's Pakistan. They looked really old. No one knew who had built their houses with these bricks, when they had done it and why they had gone away. The villagers living near one of these mysterious brick piles called it Mohenjo-daro, because in Sindhi it means, 'the mound of the dead'.

Until the 1920s no one knew that these were the remains of India's first cities and that those bricks, crumbling away in the sun, were over four thousand years old! They were still so strong that the villagers used them to build their own huts, and two British engineers happily helped themselves to a whole pile to lay the tracks for a railway line!

STOP THE FILCHING!

Then the archaeologists arrived in their khaki shorts and sola hats and yelled, 'Stop! These bricks here are very important to India's history. No more filching!' And so the sites at Harappa and Mohenjo-daro were saved. Phew! Or we would have never known about the amazing cities of the Harappan Civilization.

In the beginning the cities were called the Indus Valley Civilization, as many of the ruins are around the River Indus, but now we refer to them as the Harappan Civilization, after the first city that was discovered.

The cities and villages of the Harappan Civilization grew along the banks of one of the mighty rivers of the Indian subcontinent—the Indus or Sindhu, and its many tributaries like the Sutlej, Ravi and Ghagghar. India is named after the Indus, and here people built cities around 2600 BCE. Try to get your head around this number—*4,600 years ago!*

Cities, the first in the world, were also coming up at this time along the Euphrates and Tigris rivers in Iraq that we call the Mesopotamian or Sumerian Civilization, and along the River Nile in Egypt. This proved that India was among the oldest civilizations of the world!

The archaeologists John Marshall, Mortimer Wheeler and two young Indians, R.D. Banerji and D.R. Sahni, dug away under the burning desert sun and found much more than just bricks at Harappa. They unearthed pottery, bits of cloth, toys, jewellery, sculpture and some odd, small, square stone seals with pictures carved on them. On top of every seal is a line of script that we still can't read. From these dusty and broken finds they began to create a picture of how people lived in these cities.

In the following decades, over a thousand Harappan sites have been found, stretching from Sind to Jammu, Gujarat, Haryana and Uttar Pradesh. Mohenjo-daro, Harappa and Chanhu-daro are in Pakistan. Among the sites in India are Kalibangan (Rajasthan), Rupar (Punjab), Lothal and Dholavira (Gujarat).

COPYCAT CITIES

If you lived in Delhi and were dropped in the middle of Hyderabad, would you think they were the same? No way! Does the Marine Drive of Mumbai look the same as the Marina Beach of Chennai? Of course not! But if you lived in the Indus

Valley you could get confused because all the cities looked *pretty much the same*.

Honestly, I'm not making this up! All the cities were made using bricks that were *exactly* the same size. The streets were laid out in straight lines at right angles in an identical grid and the houses had the same design. You had two main streets, one running from north to south and another from east to west, and they were as wide as our three-lane highways.

Narrower lanes branched off from the main streets with houses on both sides. At one end of the city was a fort-like structure built on a higher ground that archaeologists call the Citadel. It had larger buildings that could have been granaries or the homes of the rulers. At points along the lanes there were wells and shady trees, and the traffic on the main roads was of people, bullock and camel carts.

BATH TIME FOLKS!

All the houses had rooms around a square courtyard and sometimes a second floor with a wooden balcony. They all looked quite the same. The houses had no windows opening into the lane, so you walked along a lot of blank walls. There were steps leading to the flat roof where people must have slept during summers like we do even today. And they were very serious about taking baths! *Every* house had a bathroom, and Mohenjo-daro had what seems to be a giant swimming pool called the Great Bath.

What is amazing is that so long ago they had planned a superb drainage system. All the waste water pouring out of houses flowed into underground drains made of giant terracotta pipes, and they even had manhole covers so that the pipes could be cleaned regularly. A sewer system does not sound very

glamorous but think about it, can a city survive without one? This is the world's first sewerage system, and building it showed great engineering skills. They also had brick garbage cans in the streets and the garbage was collected and dumped outside the city. So the streets were clean with no muddy puddles, hills of smelly garbage or open stinking drains. Don't you wish our modern Indian cities had learnt the lesson about cleanliness from Harappa?

CROCODILE CUTLET, ANYONE?

Today the Indus Valley region is a barren desert and only camels can be seen, but back then it was thickly forested and inhabited by deer, lions, tigers, leopards, rabbits, peacocks, monkeys and even rhinoceros. We know this because the animals were made into toys and their images carved on the seals. They also had bulls, buffaloes, elephants, camels and pigs.

The land was regularly flooded by the Indus that left behind a layer of silt, making the soil very fertile. The villagers grew wheat, barley, rice, chickpeas, peas, melons, dates, berries, coconut, bananas, pomegranates, garlic and other vegetables and fruits. They grew grapes, so they must have made wine. They cooked using mustard and sesame oil and ate mutton, beef, pork, fowl, fish, turtle and the meat of gharial, the crocodile with the long snout.

Wonder how they caught a gharial, with bows and arrows, spears or with nets? Now if we could decipher the Harappan script, maybe we will find the recipe for a gharial curry!

NO GHARIAL SOUP TODAY!

BANGLES AND BRACELETS

The first cotton was grown in India, and we taught the world how to weave it into cloth and then dye it in brilliant colours. Men and women in Harappa wore pretty similar clothes, so no one followed the latest fashions here! There was a strip of cloth tied at the waist like a skirt and another wrapped around the upper body. The upper cloth was brought under the right arm and thrown over the left shoulder, a bit like the sari. Needles made of bone have been found, so perhaps the women stitched blouses and embroidered them too.

The sculptures show that they liked to dress up. Both men and women kept their hair long and the women made *really* complicated hairdos—tied in big circlets above the ears, in long plaits or in huge knots on top of the head. The archaeologists found the tiny metal figurine of a young girl which was so delightful to look at that they called her the Dancing Girl. Her curled hair falls prettily across her right shoulder and she wears many bangles on her left arm, from the wrist to the shoulder, and a chunky necklace. She has a slight smile on her face, as if feeling pretty thrilled with herself, and she stands with one hand at her hip and a leg bent, almost like she is keeping beat to music.

Archaeologists have found necklaces, bangles, earrings and headbands made of beads, gold and silver, set with stones like lapis lazuli and turquoise. Also ivory combs, bronze mirrors, razors and stone jars that held make-up like kohl, henna, red rouge made of cockleshells and white and green paint.

YOU ARE LOOKING AWESOME DARLING !

LET'S PLAY!

Indians have always enjoyed gambling and playing board games. The archaeologists found dice, marbles, ivory balls and many kinds of clay toys at the Harappan sites. We don't know what the games were, because the boards made of wood have not survived, but many of the clay toys have. There are bulls on wheels, sheep with fleece painted in waves on their backs, carts with moving wheels, whistles, rattles, parrots and the cutest of all—naughty monkeys that run up and down a stick!

BEADS AND POTS

Potters, weavers, bead makers, wood carvers . . . the craftspeople all worked in the city. Villagers came to the city with grain, vegetables and fruits and returned with pots and pans, knives and ploughs. Potters used the potter's wheel and made bowls, glasses and plates, long-necked jars for storing oil and shallow pots for cooking. They painted the pots and toys with red and black patterns, with drawings of fish, birds, flowers and leaves.

Some things never change in India, and you can see similar pottery even today, just as the toy carts look exactly like the bullock carts in our villages. As the cities used a lot of bricks, kilns have been found everywhere. At one kiln rows of mud bricks left to dry in the sun show the footprints of a running cat and a dog that was chasing it.

The Harappans did not know the use of iron and only made do with copper and bronze. A bronze frying pan has been found that looks exactly like the ones we use to fry omelettes. It is also known that there were jewellers making gold and silver bangles, earrings and necklaces. Some of the bead necklaces show they knew how to polish precious stones and pierce them to make necklaces. As no coins have been found, historians think that trade must have been through the barter system.

YOU THE KING, ARE YOU?

Such well-run cities must have had very strict and efficient governments that could make the people obey the laws. But strangely, no temples, palaces or royal tombs have been found. Mesopotamia had magnificent temples and we know of Egyptian kings because they were buried in pyramids. Did that mean the Harappans did not have kings? As we can't read the script we can only guess, and no sculpture shows a king wearing a crown or waving a sword. Historians, guessing a bit, think they may have been ruled by priests. So it means they had a theocracy, not a monarchy.

The historians came to this conclusion because of a single image of a grim-looking man wearing a flowered robe. He has a decorated diadem tied around his forehead and a kind of I-am-very-important look on his face. Historians call him the High Priest. He looks back at you with heavy lidded eyes and thick lips that do not smile, like a disapproving judge. Even four thousand years later he is a bit scary.

HOW DID THEY PRAY?

Even today Indian temples, especially in South India, have a large pool for people to bathe in. The Great Bath at Mohenjo-daro may have similarly been part of a temple complex where these ruler-priests lived. But where are the images of the gods and goddesses they worshipped? It might be possible that the images were made of wood and so haven't survived. There are also these clay figures of plump women wearing fan-shaped headdresses and necklaces that historians think were worshipped as the Mother Goddess.

Then there is that mysterious thin man carved on seals. He sits cross-legged wearing a buffalo horn headdress, a bit like the ones some tribal people wear when they dance. What is interesting is that he is often shown surrounded by animals. As we know, one of the names of Lord Shiva is Pashupati, lord of the animals, and he always sits cross-legged. So it is assumed that the man carved on seals is an early form of Shiva.

THE MYSTERIOUS SEALS

Most of the seals are the size of large postage stamps and made of a stone called steatite. One side has carvings and a line of script on top. The most beautiful show a bull with curving horns, a big hump and heavy dewlaps, a rhinoceros and a one-horned antelope. The script on top is actually a pictorial one, with funny curves and zigzags. We have collected around 500 symbols of the script that still puzzles us, and they could be alphabets or complete words. Scholars trying to crack the code have even used computer programmes, but it hasn't solved the mystery.

What perplexes historians even more is why the seals were made and how they were used. Historians make wild guesses again—they were stamps for sealing bags and packets for trading; they were identity cards carried by officials; or they were symbols of families . . . It would all become clear the moment we decipher the script.

TO THE GULF

Harappan seals have been found at ancient Mesopotamian cities like Ur, proving that they traded with each other. Harappan ships must have sailed from Lothal in Gujarat and gone across the Arabian Sea to the ports of the Gulf. They also traded by land with other regions, getting precious stones and metals from Afghanistan, jade from China, gold and ivory from South India. Their biggest export was of woven cotton.

We call these Harappan cities by their modern names, but we don't know what they were originally called. Luckily, the Mesopotamian script has been deciphered and they mention three places in the east they traded with—Meluha, Dilmun and Makan. So could Mohenjo-daro possibly be Meluha? Don't you wish the historians would hurry up and crack the script so that all this guessing could stop?

HARAPPA? NEVER HEARD OF IT!

After a thousand years, the cities began to die around 1500 BCE. Archaeologists think there was a change in the environment. First the forests were completely wiped out, and then the rivers like the Ghagghar began to dry up and the land turned into a desert. There are also signs of flooding, on the walls of houses. So it is possible that the Indus changed its course and flooded the cities. The Harappan Civilization is perhaps the earliest examples of an environmental disaster because of deforestation.

Today the Indus flows far away from these cities, so it may have moved away and water became scarce.

What is very interesting is that very few weapons have been found, proving the Harappans were a peaceful people. Moreover, the weapons were made of bronze and not as strong as those made of iron. They did not even have horses which were essential in ancient warfare. So a more aggressive people riding horses and chariots, and using iron weapons, had an advantage over the Harappans. When the tribes of the Indo-Aryan people began to enter India from Afghanistan, they could have conquered the Harappans very easily.

The oldest book of the Aryans is the Rig Veda, and its poems talk about their gods defeating cities. So the cities destroyed by the vajra thunderbolts of the Aryan god Indra may have been those of the Harappan Civilization. The Aryans were nomads and didn't settle down in villages or build cities. Thus the next cities would only be built nearly a thousand years later. After the Harappan cities were abandoned by their citizens, no new cities rose and Mohenjo-daro and Harappa were forgotten.

THE INDO-ARYANS
(1500 BCE—500 BCE)

A DAY IN THE LIFE OF DHANI

As the sun rose above the horizon, Dhani and his father left their thatched hut and walked to their fields at the end of the village. Dhani's father was leading their bull and he was carrying the plough.

Lord Indra, the god who brought rain, had been kind to them this year; the monsoons had come on time and they were busy ploughing and sowing. They were going to plant wheat and barley, and soon the rains would flood the fields and the plants would grow tall, green and abundant with grains.

As their bull pulled, his father pushed the wooden plough deep into the brown muddy earth and Dhani walked behind him scattering the seeds into the furrow. All the while he sang a song of thanksgiving in praise of Lord Indra, praying for rain to give them green grass that would fatten their cattle. As he looked up and saw the dark grey clouds scudding across the sky, Dhani's heart sang with happiness. This year they would eat well, he hoped.

'I think Lord Indra deserves a new song,' thought Dhani, 'not this old one I have been singing for years.' He was good at rhyming, and the first two lines came to him quickly. As he walked along, his feet sinking into the soft, loamy earth, Dhani softly whispered the words of the new song in his head:

> 'Oh my dear Lord Indra, O great warrior,
> I praise thee with every splash of rain.'

Dhani remembered how Lord Indra, who was the commander of the army of the gods, always carried a thunderbolt called Vajra.

> 'As your Vajra thunderbolt streaks across the sky,
> The greatest of the gods you remain.'

SOMEONE PLEASE STOP THIS POET!!

The next two lines came easily because he knew what Lord Indra liked to be offered at the sacrifices.

> 'I will worship thee mighty Lord Indra,
> With flowers, fruits and the new harvest's grain.'

'Two more lines I think ...' Dhani said looking up as a flock of snow white geese flew in neat rows across the grey sky. And the last two lines came floating into his mind:

> 'Like the geese flying across the sky,
> Ride back on the grey clouds again!'

◆ ◆ ◆

Like Dhani, many Aryans were poets singing their prayers to their gods, and these hymns are what we find in the Vedas.

As the cities of the Harappan Civilization slowly vanished, a new group of people were entering India. They called themselves the Arya, which means kinsman or companion, and we know them as the Aryans. Historians think they were nomadic tribes that moved from Central Asia into Iran and then through Afghanistan into India. Starting around 1500 BC they entered the Indian subcontinent in many waves.

The Aryans, with huge herds of cattle and sheep, were constantly on the move in search of fresh pasture. Their life was very different from those of the sophisticated city dwellers of Mohenjo-daro and Harappa. As they were always travelling, they did not build stone or brick houses but temporary thatched huts. They did not have temples and prayed to their gods by lighting a fire under the open sky. Most importantly, they did not have a written language and no system of trading in goods with other regions. It was a much simpler and more rural life.

While exploring Harappa, the archaeologists had lots of fun digging up things as they had whole cities to explore, only they

could not read the
script. In the case
of the Aryans, there
was little to dig up
except some pottery,
but they composed a lot of religious
poems or shlokas that were later
written down. So the ancient Aryans
speak to us through their prayers and
hymns, mantras and magic spells, and
by studying them the historians can
recreate a picture of their lives.

SIR, NO SIGNS
OF ARYANS
DOWN HERE!

The Aryans have given us our oldest
book, the amazing Rig Veda, and after it
came three others—Sam Veda, Atharva Veda and Yajur Veda.
Then there are the philosophical writings of the Upanishads and
two fabulous epic tales—the Ramayana and the Mahabharata.
We have to piece our history together from the works of poets,
philosophers, teachers and storytellers. Thus, this period whose
history is based on the Vedas, is also called the Vedic Age.

MEMORY MAGIC

Whenever anyone says 'Veda' we think of this fat book with a
dull brown cover, filled with lines in Sanskrit that are very hard
to understand. The Vedas are in fact collections of prayers and
hymns in praise of gods and goddesses, and many of them are
really beautiful to read. What's more, they were not just solemn
prayers; there are funny rhymes about frogs croaking in the
monsoons, poems about love and anger and most amusing, the
lament of a stupid man who has lost all his money gambling.

The Gayatri Mantra, 'Om bhur bhuvasva . . .' that many of you
may have learnt, is in praise of Surya, the sun god. And here is
a poem praising Ushas, the beautiful goddess of dawn:

'See how the dawn has set up her banner,
Glowing across the eastern sky.
O my goddess Ushas, adorning us with a golden sunlight.'

The word 'vidya' or knowledge comes from the word 'veda', and most of these poems or shlokas were composed by scholars called rishis, like Vishwamitra, Bharadwaja and Atri. Some are by women sages like Gargi and Maitreyi. The Rig Veda has over two thousand shlokas and the other three Vedas are a mix of prayers, rules of sacrifice and magic spells including some weird ones like a spell against snakebite. Considering the fact that snakes did not know any Sanskrit, it is doubtful if it worked! There are also some pretty mind-blowing curses to be used against enemies. Imagine cursing in Sanskrit and saying 'Gardhabhasya samoh buddhihi tave' (you have the brains of a donkey)!

In the beginning these poems were not written down but memorized by the priests called Brahmins. Yes! Thousands of shlokas were learnt by heart just like your multiplication tables, and young Brahmin boys would repeat them endlessly. There was a system to it, as different Brahmin families would memorize different sections. In this way the Vedas were kept alive by generations of Brahmins, through hundreds of years, in what is called an oral tradition.

IT LOOKS LIKE
MY SPELL AGAINST
SNAKE BITE IS
NOT WORKING!!

The boys first learnt to read, write, do some simple arithmetic and then got down to memorizing the shlokas to be recited at religious ceremonies. It wasn't easy because you had to pronounce every word correctly and Sanskrit has some pretty tongue-twisting words! They believed that if you mispronounced a mantra, the gods would curse you. So if you made a mistake, your teacher would definitely give you a whack with his stick.

PRIESTS, WARRIORS AND FARMERS

The Aryans gradually began to settle down in villages, cleared out the forests and started growing crops. The Aryan tribes were often at war with one another as they kept stealing each other's cattle. The most powerful tribes were the Bharatas—that's how India came to be known as Bharat. Some of the others were Puru, Kuru, Panchal, Madra and Gandhar, and if their names sound familiar it's because they all fought at Kurukshetra in the Mahabharata.

The warriors who protected the tribe called themselves the Kshatriyas. The most powerful Kshatriya became the chieftain, called Rajan, and he called the Brahmins to recite prayers before a battle. The priests would build a fire, pour ghee into it and sing the mantras. Then they would sacrifice an ox or sheep and everyone would have a feast. This ceremony was called a yagya. The real hard work of growing crops was done by the farmers, who were called Vaishyas. And the craftspeople weaving cloth, making earthen pots or carving wood were called the Shudras.

As the Brahmins and the Kshatriyas were the most powerful, they called themselves the upper classes or varnas; in the later centuries these divisions of society became fixed. However, in the early days it was not so rigid; a varna just described the work you did and you were free to change your profession. A Kshatriya could compose shlokas and a Vaishya could become a warrior. There is a song where the writer says that he is a poet, his father is a physician and his mother grinds corn. So unlike what Hindus believe today, varna or caste was not hereditary.

OH VARUNA, LISTEN TO ME!

So who were these gods and goddesses the Aryans prayed to? There was Indra, carrying a thunderbolt, god of thunder and rain. He was the commander of the army of the gods and always fighting demons. Agni was the god of fire, and they prayed to him during a yagya. Yama was the god of death, Prithvi, the earth goddess, and Surya, the divine sun. Varuna was a sort of celestial judge who watched humans from the sky and punished evil people. The beautiful Ushas was the goddess of dawn, and Aranyani, the goddess of the forests.

The strangest god was Soma; it was actually a divine drink that was said to give immortality. This intoxicating drink produced hallucinations and it was made by crushing a plant and mixing it with milk. It was drunk during yagyas. We still don't know exactly what that mysterious Soma plant was, as the Vedas don't describe it.

It seems deities can also go out of fashion! Many of the gods and goddesses of the Rig Veda are no longer popular with the Hindus. There are no temples to Indra or Varuna; Ushas and Aranyani have been forgotten, while gods like Vishnu and Shiva, who were not known during Vedic times, are now worshipped everywhere.

A FARMING LIFE

Aryan villages were clusters of houses surrounded by fields, and thick forests lay beyond. They built an earthen wall around the village to keep out wild animals like elephants, tigers and leopards that would come out of the forests. They were organic farmers, using natural fertilizers and making sure the soil was never spoilt.

The richest man in a group of villages was the Kshatriya chieftain or Rajan, and he liked to show off by performing elaborate yagyas like the Rajasuya and Ashwamedha. The Rajasuya yagya celebrated the coronation of a king. The Ashwamedha yagya was a horse sacrifice. A horse was set free to roam and if it entered another kingdom, the king of that region could either fight or offer tribute to the king who owned the horse. The priests were rewarded with gold, clothes and land. So if the hymns are always full of praise of the Kshatriyas, it is because the writer was a priest glorifying his rich patron. The yagyas would go on for days, with dozens of priests filling the air with their droning chants as they poured lots of ghee into the sacred fire. They were big, noisy affairs with animals being sacrificed and the guests would then be treated to a feast.

GROWING UP

I DIDN'T BREAK IT MAA!

Aryan families were just like our joint families—parents, grandparents, siblings, uncles, aunts and cousins all living under one roof. Fathers were pretty strict and there are many stories of punishment for disobedient children. The mothers ran the homes—cooking, cleaning, weaving cloth and going to the river or well to collect water. Men made

ATITHI DEVA BHAVA!

their living as farmers or craftsmen like carpenters, potters, basket makers, ironsmiths, hunters, and also as charioteers, astrologers and jewellers. Once the boys grew up, they helped their fathers and the girls worked at home. Learning to read and write was not considered very important for most people except the Brahmins.

We have a saying, 'Atithi deva bhava'—a guest is like a god—and the Aryans were really kind and hospitable people. Guests were welcomed into the home and given the best food to eat and a place to stay. Of course we don't know what they did with the pesky guest who refused to leave! Their entertainment was simple—singing and dancing, playing flutes, conches, cymbals and drums during festivals and weddings. The children played with marbles, toys and board games. The men gambled with dice, and everyone would gather to watch chariot races.

BEING A GIRL

All the prayers in the Vedas begging for children ask for boys, and that says it all. Being a woman meant you had to be obedient to men—father, brothers, husband and even sons. One of the Vedas says, 'A good woman is one who pleases her husband, delivers male children and never talks back to her husband.' So, basically shut up and behave yourself.

Women had no right to own anything beyond what they got in marriage, called stridhan, but still they had more freedom in this era than in the later periods. They moved about quite freely; in fact poems describe them going to markets, dressing up and enjoying festivals, and there was no system of wearing veils. They were married only after they reached their teens, widows were allowed to remarry and some girls even chose their own husbands and eloped!

The Rig Veda mentions a woman sage called Ghosha who stayed single, and two others, Gargi and Maitreyi, who wrote hymns. It is said that Gargi once stood up in public and argued about philosophy with a rishi called Yagnyavalkya. She asked such difficult questions that he finally lost his temper and threatened to curse her if she did not shut up! Women teachers were called brahmavadinis, and the Mahabharata says Draupadi was a scholar who supervised the accounts of the kingdom. Likewise, Apala became a farmer, Vishpala, Mudgalini and Vadhrimati became warriors. But you have to remember that these women are mentioned by name in the books only because it was so rare.

THERE WAS A BRAVE PRINCE . . .

Storytellers, called sutas, travelled from village to village with their bagfuls of stories about kings and jesters, battles, romances, ghosts and demons. We should say a big thank you to these sutas because they kept alive two of our greatest epics—the Ramayana and the Mahabharata.

The word 'suta' also means a charioteer, many of them took part in battles and described these wars like the Mahabharata. The epics are not just tales; they are a bit of our history and the people in them are very like us. There is brave Arjuna and cruel Duryodhana, beautiful Sita and proud Draupadi, loyal Hanuman and Yudhisthira, who could not resist gambling. Their stories are our roots and they give us the traditions that make us Indians.

When a suta arrived in a village, he would be welcomed into the chieftain's house and there would be a feast in his honour. Then as the sun began to dip below the horizon, people would gather around him as he sat beside a tall earthen lamp and began his story, of Sita's swayamvara in the Ramayana or the gambling scene in the Mahabharata. He would recite poems, act out the scene with dialogues and at times even spring up and dance. That is how our traditional theatre began, like the Ram Leela, Yakshagana and Kathakali.

FEASTING AND FASTING

How do we know what the Aryans ate? Simple! In their hymns, they offered their best foods to the gods. Sort of 'Dear Lord Indra, have a bowl of payasam with raisins and then please answer my prayers.' Hindus do it still, offering a prasad of bananas and sweets to the deity when they do puja. The feasts had a menu cooked in fragrant ghee and spices, and many such dishes find mention in the sacred books. The earliest dishes that are mentioned are—apupa, barley cooked in ghee; odana made with grain, milk, curd and ghee; and karambha which seems to be a kind of porridge.

Recipe of Apupa
- Make a thick batter of rice or barley flour.
- Heat ghee in a flat pan.
- Pour a ladle of the batter and fry.
- Dip fried apupa in honey.

You can still eat apupas. It is the Bengali malpua dripping in sugar syrup, totally yum!

As the Aryans moved eastward from the Punjab, through Haryana to the banks of the River Ganga, they discovered many new kinds of grains, vegetables and fruits. In the beginning they mostly ate barley (called yava), but now they began to grow wheat (godhuma) and rice (vrihi) which became their main cereal. That must have been quite a relief for the Aryan kids... Imagine barley for breakfast, lunch and dinner!

The dish most often offered to the gods was kshira: rice boiled in milk and sweetened with honey or sugar and perked up with raisins. We call it kheer in the north and payasam in the south. We still eat many of the Aryan dishes and among them is vataka, or the vada! Wheat was ground, kneaded and made into rotis. Rice was mixed with moong or masoor dal and cooked with spices as a khichri. Rice simply boiled in water was bhataka and flattened rice was called chipitika, what we call chivda.

The Aryans were cattle owners, so milk and milk products like curd, butter and ghee were an important part of their diet. The most precious milk product was of course ghee (ghrita). Curd was churned with honey and milk and made into delicious lassi. Another curd dessert was shirkarini and that was our shrikhand of course. One poem describes two milk products that are with and without holes, but does not give their names. Do you think that was cottage cheese, what we call paneer, and proper cured cheese that has holes? An Aryan cheddar or gouda would be interesting!

The Aryan basket of vegetables and fruits was getting bigger. Berries, dates, musk and watermelons, coconut, bananas and mangoes are mentioned, as are cucumbers, lotus roots, gourds, radish, garlic and ginger. Aryan mothers must have yelled at their children to make them eat a gourd called karavella. You guessed it right—it is our bitter gourd or karela! They were crunching large, crispy parpatas with their rice and dal, and we call them papad. They also ate meat, poultry, deer, rabbit, crab, turtles and fish.

They were very good at brewing wine called sura made from grapes, sugar cane or rice and flavoured with fruits, spices and flowers. One scholar, who must have enjoyed his drink, has taken the trouble of making a list of thirty kinds of wine with poetic names like madhira, varuni and prasanna. Mahasura was a mango juice wine, and the drink offered to honoured guests was called madhuparka. Actually it doesn't sound that tasty, being a mix of ghee, curd, milk, honey and sugar!

DRESSING UP

The clothes that the Aryans wore were simple: just a lower garment called vasa and an upper garment called adivasa, made of cotton or wool. These were long strips of cloth wrapped, tied and pleated in various ways. They dressed up by wearing gold and silver jewellery, with both men and women wearing bangles, earrings, necklaces, rings and anklets. They kept their hair long, oiled and combed, and men wore turbans. Women tied their hair in elaborate hairdos and one poem describes a girl with her hair tied in four plaits. They all loved flowers, wearing fragrant jasmine garlands around their necks, tied around their wrists and wrapped into their hair.

TWO: ANCIENT INDIA

The Mauryas and Guptas
The Pallavas and Cholas

The Mauryas and Guptas
(300 BCE–500 CE)

A DAY IN THE LIFE OF MADHURA

Madhura stood before her mistress, holding the bronze mirror as the princess put on her make-up. Another maid was combing her hair, tying it in a low bun and putting in gold hairpins with tiny bells attached to them. The princess lined her eyes with kohl and then drew an intricately designed tikka on her forehead with vermilion.

Madhura gave a small sigh and thought, what a boring way to live, spending hours just dressing up every day. If she had been a princess, she would have gone riding and learnt to fight with a sword. It would be so much more interesting than being a princess' maid and holding a mirror for hours.

Madhura couldn't stop herself from yawning and the princess looked up at her with a frown, 'What's the matter?'

'Nothing, Your Highness,' Madhura said quickly.

'Our Madhura is not interested in clothes or make-up,' the maid said teasingly. 'She gets bored working here.'

'Really? Then what do you want to do?' the princess asked with a smile. 'Cook? Sew clothes? Weave?'

'No!' Madhura shook her curly head. 'All girls do that! I want to ride horses and fight with swords . . .'

Both the women began to laugh, 'Girls don't do that, Madhura,' the princess said kindly.

'Of course they do!' Madhura said hotly. 'His Majesty, our king Ashoka, is guarded by women soldiers and they carry swords, spears and daggers *and* they ride beside his chariot. I want to be like them.'

'Then you shall become a soldier,' said a deep male voice behind her, making Madhura turn in surprise. King Ashoka was standing with an amused smile on his dark, sharp-featured face.

'Your Majesty!' Madhura bowed in panic. 'I did not . . . I mean . . .'

A gentle hand ruffled her hair. 'Come with me Madhura, my warrior girl. I'll make you a fighter one day.'

'Oh yes, Your Majesty!' grinned Madhura, and turning to the maid she handed the mirror to her. 'Keep it. I won't need it any more!' Then she looked up at the kind face of her gentle king, 'I'm ready Your Majesty!'

King Ashoka and Princess Sanghamitra laughed.

Madhura lived in Pataliputra, in the palace of King Ashoka of the Mauryan dynasty. Ashoka ruled over one of the greatest empires of the ancient world.

In 324 BCE, a warrior named Chandragupta Maurya conquered the mighty kingdom of Magadha that was ruled by the Nanda kings from their capital city of Pataliputra. Chandragupta, his son Bindusara and his grandson Ashoka built the first Indian empire whose borders stretched from Bihar to Afghanistan. Ashoka is remembered even today because he became a Buddhist, gave up wars and chose non-violence at a time when kings were expected to be ruthless conquerors.

The next powerful kingdom in north India was that of the Guptas, who ruled between 322 and 547 CE. Just to confuse us, that dynasty had two kings who were also called Chandragupta. The three most powerful Gupta kings were therefore Chandragupta I, Samudragupta and Chandragupta II Vikramaditya. These three Gupta kings ruled over a kingdom where there was prosperity and great progress in art and architecture. Some of the most beautiful sculptures came from the workshops of Mathura, and we began building stone temples and monasteries.

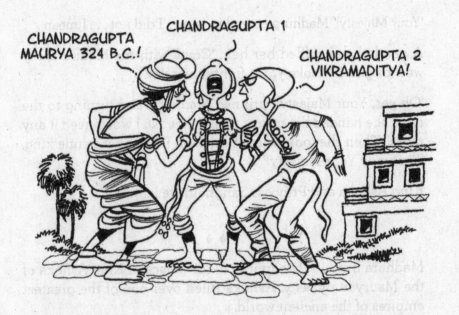

In this section we are taking the Mauryas and the Guptas together, which is a span of about 800 years, because even though there were many upheavals in the political scene, the life of the people moved smoothly along similar paths and there were no drastic changes in people's daily lives.

Now it is easier to create a portrait of people's lives because there are many books like Kautilya's *Arthashastra*, the poetry and plays of Kalidas, the plays of Bhasa, Vatsayana's *Kamasutra*, the Jataka stories of the Buddhists and the *Panchatantra* tales of Vishnu Sharma. We also have the accounts of travellers like Megasthenes who came to Pataliputra as the ambassador of the Greek king Seleukos Nikator. He stayed in India for many years, travelled widely around the kingdom of Magadha and wrote a book called *Indica*.

Buddhism was very popular and many Indians had become Buddhists. The religion spread to Sri Lanka, Tibet and China and pilgrims came to India to visit monasteries and study at Buddhist universities like Nalanda and Taxila. They wrote about their experiences, like Fa Xian who came during the reign of

Chandragupta II, and Huan Tsang who arrived at the court of King Harsha in the 7th century CE.

THE TAXMAN IS HERE!

It was a green land made up of villages and forests with only a few towns and cities in between. Village life had this eternal air, with farmers bent over their ploughs and potters moulding pots with muddy hands over their spinning wooden wheels. Weavers worked at their looms and women spun cotton thread, wove mats and baskets and children herded cows and goats in the meadows. Villages had houses made of thatched roofs and mud brick walls, and a temple; water was collected from rivers, ponds and wells. The Mauryan government had become well organized and the king taxed his subjects. Farmers were expected to pay a part of their crops to the royal tax collector. You can be sure these taxmen were not very popular with the farmers!

There was a large tribal population called Shabaras and Aranyacharas. They lived in the forests and often came into conflict with villagers who cut down trees to clear the land for growing crops. The tribals too had to pay taxes, and gave the products of the forest like honey, herbal plants, animal skins, elephants, metals and timber to the government. Tribal warriors were recruited for the army during wars as they were very skilled with their bows and arrows.

I LOVE PATALIPUTRA

There were large cities like Pataliputra, Ujjain, Taxila, Kannauj, Kashi, and sea ports like Tamralipti and Bharukachha. Megasthenes has given a detailed description of Pataliputra (modern Patna), which was a magnificent city of palaces and gardens, busy bazaars and a cosmopolitan courtly life. Most cities were built beside a river, like Varanasi and Pataliputra were beside the River Ganga, and there was much traffic of boats carrying goods to the markets. The city roads were noisy with the clip-clop of horses' hooves, swaying elephants, the rattle of bullock carts, chariots and palanquin bearers yelling at pedestrians to move away. They did not have the police to handle traffic jams as cart drivers argued with horse riders or an elephant refused to move!

It was said that Pataliputra never slept. The city was protected by a high wall made of giant logs of wood. Some of these logs on the walls of Ashoka's palace were discovered in the twentieth century when sewers were being dug in Patna! Soldiers marched day and night on top of the wall and there were narrow slits from where they aimed arrows and spears. There was a broad moat outside, and at night the moat bridges were raised and the gates closed so no one could enter the city. Only the royal spies knew of secret underground tunnels as they often came in the night to report to the king.

The cities were planned in such a way that each profession, like the clans of weavers or jewellers, lived in one locality, and there were temples and monasteries, bazaars, food shops and

??!!

PATALIPUTRA NEVER SLEEPS!

inns. Shops sold clothes, perfumes and jewellery, foodgrains, garlands, fruits, vegetables, pottery, metalware and woodcraft. At the heart of the city stood the fortress where the royal family had their palaces and also offices. The nobility built their mansions around the palace that was surrounded by a wall and guarded by soldiers. So for an ordinary citizen to try to meet a prince or royal official was as difficult as it is for us to meet a minister or a bureaucrat today.

The mansions of the rich were made of wood and brick and some were three storeys high, while the poor lived in single-roomed thatched huts. The walls of the mansions were made of brick, whitewashed and decorated with paintings. The rooms were placed around an open courtyard with trees, and a pillared veranda ran around it. Rooms had polished red tiled floors, windows swaying with curtains, and cages full of chattering birds hung in the veranda. Some of the rich folk had bathrooms with running water, not through taps of course; instead a channel brought water from the river or stream.

Cities had parks, lotus pools and bathing tanks and the rich had their own gardens, vines of scented flowers and fish ponds. The poet Kalidas describes a machine that spurted water to cool a courtyard, similar to the sprinkler system we use to water lawns today. The gardens had swings hanging from trees and many romantic poems describe women swinging on them exactly like we see in our films.

Homes were furnished with carved wood furniture, soft cushions, carpets, curtains and were lit by oil lamps. The rich led a life of leisure as they owned large estates and only a few men were ambitious enough to become ministers in the government or joined the army. The idle young men played musical instruments like the veena, read palm leaf books, painted and composed poetry. They attended musical soirées where courtesans sang and poets recited their compositions.

I LISTENED TO YOUR POEMS! NOW IT'S YOUR TURN TO LISTEN TO MINE!!

Sanskrit and Tamil literature is full of tales about these lazy men about town, who seemed to have nothing to do except romance women and fall crazily in love.

VARNA, JATI, GOTRA PLEASE

By now the divisions of society according to varna had become quite rigid. The four main varnas of Brahmin, Kshatriya, Vaishya and Shudra did not intermarry or even eat together. Below them were the outcastes—the untouchables who were forced to live outside towns and villages. Then the varnas became subdivided into jatis and further into gotras. It became so confusing that Megasthenes thought there were seven varnas! Later the Portuguese called the varnas *castas* or tribes. Thus the English word we use today—caste—comes from the Portuguese word for tribe!

Brahmins were teachers, priests, advisers to kings and also astrologers. They were often called to use their mantras and magic spells. However, the real power and money was in the hands of the Kshatriyas, who were the kings, army generals and ministers. By now the Vaishyas had become very rich by trading with the Roman Empire. Traders travelled along the two main highways, the Dakshinapatha that led to the ports of Gujarat, and the Uttarapatha that led to the Silk Route. The Silk Route was the land route travelled by traders, connecting China and India to Europe through Afghanistan, Persia and the Middle East. The traders resented the fact that even though they were well off, the power remained in the hands of the Brahmins and Kshatriyas. Hence, many of them became Buddhists because in Buddhism there were no castes and everyone was equal.

The Shudras were the craftsmen and they too were becoming prosperous as products like textiles, pottery, stone carving and metalware were being traded to other countries. The Mauryan red and black pottery was famous, as were the woven cottons of the east. In fact by the time of the Guptas, they had become skilled at using iron to make pots, tools and weapons. One example of their skill is the Iron Pillar at Delhi that stands before the Qutab Minar. It was probably made during the reign of Chandragupta II and has not rusted even after so many centuries.

Even so, people did choose professions that were out of their varna. We read of Brahmin and Vaishya kings and Shudra traders; Brahmin farmers, Kshatriya potters and garland makers. However, the fate of the untouchable seldom changed as they did all the dirty, menial work. They were the cobblers, fishermen, sweepers and hunters. The men who worked with leather were called chandals and were considered the lowest of the outcastes even though their goods, like shoes and sandals, water bags and saddles, were used by everyone. The Brahmins considered even their shadow to be defiling, and a chandal had to warn people when he entered a village by hitting two pieces of stick. This absurd obsession with 'purity' meant that upper-class Hindus considered everyone else as 'impure'; in fact even foreigners were called mlechhas and they refused to share a meal with them.

Megasthenes wrote that India did not have any slaves, but he was mistaken. People did have slaves called dasas. Some were children of slaves, others prisoners of war or people who had sold themselves into slavery for a limited time to pay off a debt; most of them worked in households. There were laws about the proper treatment of slaves and legal ways in which they could gain their freedom.

TEMPLES AND MONASTERIES

Hindus no longer followed the old tradition of yagyas and animal sacrifices. Instead they visited temples with images of deities where they prayed with flowers and food. The old deities like Indra and Varuna were forgotten and Vishnu, Shiva and the Devi were worshipped. The biggest change was the appearance of two new religions that rejected the varna system and sacrifices, and spoke of equality and non-violence—Buddhism and Jainism. The two great teachers—Gautama Buddha and Vardhaman Mahavira—offered a new lease of life to people oppressed by the upper castes.

Now towns and villages had monasteries, and Buddhist and Jain monks became part of the life of the people. Every morning the saffron-robed monks would wander from door to door begging for food, and even if the family was Hindu, the housewife would give him a handful of rice. In the same way, boys would learn to read and write at the temple or monastery school, and men would go and ask the advice of the priests and monks or get medicines from them. People from every religion would gather and enjoy festivals and religious ceremonies like we do today.

GROWING UP

People lived in large joint families and as polygamy was common, children would often have stepmothers. Boys helped their fathers, while girls helped the women with the housework and a few of them even went to school. Only Brahmin and Kshatriya boys were educated. Sometimes the daughters of rich families were taught at home, but only enough to read the sacred books and do some basic arithmetic so that they could run the household.

There were schools run by Brahmin teachers or Buddhist monks and many different subjects were taught. The Brahmin was the guru and the boys were his shishyas; the guru had to accept whatever his students gave as fees or dakshina. So a rich student's father could gift land, gold, cows or horses, but the fees could also be simple things like shoes, grain, umbrellas, vegetables or clothes.

Most of the time was spent in memorizing the sacred texts, apart from learning mathematics, grammar, logic, astronomy and poetry. But strangely, geography, physics or chemistry was not taught at all. Higher studies included medicine and philosophy, and one of the greatest centres of learning was the University of Nalanda in Bihar which was founded by the Gupta kings. People came from other countries to study here, and admission was so tough that only two or three out of ten applicants were accepted.

NO FUN BEING A GIRL

Apart from King Ashoka, no one thought much of women. Ashoka even appointed a minister for their welfare called—now try to say this fast—stri-adhyaksha-mahamatra! This minister helped poor women get work and took care of widows and old women. But overall, the status of women was getting worse and girls were married off at a much younger age. Girls had to be docile and obedient, and as the men married many times, a wife had no power at home and widows were not allowed to remarry. Then there were scholars like Manu, who clearly did not approve of women. He wrote pompously, 'She should do nothing independently even in her own house. In childhood subject to her father, in youth to her husband and when her husband is dead to her son. She should never enjoy independence.' Over the centuries men have found the sayings of Manu very useful when they treated their wives badly or refused to share the family property with their sisters.

Fortunately, the custom of seclusion or zenana was not very rigid and women did not veil themselves. This we know from the sculptures of couples where the woman stands beside her husband wearing lots of jewellery and a happy smile. As one reads in poems and plays, women especially of poor families, moved about freely and mixed with men. The king probably kept his women in the harem and the nobility did the same, but even these women did not stay secluded all the time and did

move out without veils. There are descriptions of royal women drinking wine at parties and conversing with men.

Even so, many women did find ways to be independent. Prabhavati Gupta, the daughter of Chandragupta II, ruled the Vakataka kingdom as a regent for her young son. Vijayabhattarika, a princess of the Chalukyan dynasty that ruled in the Deccan in the 7th century CE, was the governor of a province. Interestingly, kings kept women guards around them as they were thought to be more loyal and trustworthy than men. These women warriors wore trousers and tunics and carried a spear, shield and sword. They checked the king's food, served him wine and carried him to his apartments when he was tired.

There were women scholars and teachers called upadhyayis. Many of them escaped their miserable lives by joining the Buddhist Sangha as nuns and spent their lives in study and prayers. There is a collection of poems called *Therigatha*, the song of the nuns, and it is the oldest anthology of women's writing in the world.

This poem by Sumangalamata captures their feeling:

'A woman's well set free! How free I am.
How wonderfully free, from kitchen drudgery.
Free from the harsh grip of hunger and from empty
    cooking pots.
Free too of that unscrupulous man, the weaver of sunshades.'
            (translated by Uma Chakravarty and Kumkum Roy)

Interestingly, the most cultured and independent women were courtesans or ganikas. They were educated, learnt music and dance, wrote poetry and painted. They lived on their own, managed their own money and some of them became very rich. They held art exhibitions and young noblemen were sent to them to learn cultured behaviour. Many courtesans acted as spies for the king, reporting what the rich men talked about at their musical soirées!

PANCHAGAVYA, ANYONE?

As people moved east, newer vegetables and fruits were added to the food basket. For example peaches, apricots and plums appeared, and mangoes became so popular they were praised in poems. Rice became the main staple of the diet as wheat was not so popular and was usually eaten by the poor. A particular variety of rice grown in Magadha, called Mahashali, was so precious that only royalty was allowed to eat it. People also learnt to chew paan and the habit may have come from the South. Paan was called tambula in Sanskrit, and courtesans are described as offering them to their guests.

It was believed that a balanced meal should have six pure tastes—sweet, sour, salty, pungent, bitter and astringent. A new belief prevailed that curdling milk to make cottage cheese was not healthy, so only curd, ghee and cream were made from milk. The Aryans were very fond of a drink called madhuparka. Now another holy liquid used in religious purification ceremonies was made from the products of the cow called panchagavya, and it had milk, curd, ghee and also urine and dung ... Eeeuw! There is even mention of people eating peacocks, hedgehogs, porcupine, iguana and rhinoceros!

By now there was regular trade with South India and cooks had spices like pepper, cardamom, cloves, fenugreek, cumin, coriander and mustard in their kitchens. Also, with the greater use of iron there were many kinds of pans, bowls, ladles, frying spoons and spatulas in the kitchen. Megasthenes observed the eating habits of Indians and wrote, 'They have no fixed hours when meals are to be taken by all in common, but each one eats when he feels inclined.'

The influence of Jainism and Buddhism led to many becoming vegetarians, and the Brahmins also followed the tradition. For some strange reason the Saraswat Brahmins of Karnataka and those of Bengal and Kashmir remained non-vegetarians and are so till today.

MAURYAN COUTURE

Through the reigns of the Mauryans and the Guptas, the prosperity of the people grew and so did their passion for fashion. The idle rich spent most of their time dressing up to sally out to dance and musical performances, smelling of jasmines and sandal. Weavers produced cotton as thin as gossamer and the most famous place for woven cottons was Kashi (modern Varanasi). Even two thousand years later, its weavers are still creating magic with cottons, silks and gold thread. Lord Buddha's shroud was made by the weavers of Kashi, and in medieval times the poet-philosopher Kabir was a weaver by profession.

There is a full-size stone statue of a woman called the Didargunj Yakshi that is a model of Mauryan fashion. The curvaceous woman, who smiles flirtatiously, wears an intricately pleated dhoti, and the wrap for her upper body is draped casually over an arm. There are huge, round anklets drooping over her feet and her hair, forehead, waist, arms and neck are loaded with jewellery.

The lower garment, pleated and draped in many intricate ways, was called the antariya and over it sometimes women tied a jewelled belt called mekhala. The upper garment, called uttariya, was like a shawl or dupatta and was draped in various ways—wrapped over the shoulders, folded under the right arm or drooping over the chest. By the time of the Guptas many kinds of stitched clothes were also worn, like a short blouse called cholaka or kanchuka and pleated skirts by the women, while men wore long kurta-style tunics. The clothes of the rich were often covered in embroidery or decorated with pearls and gems.

For men, turbans and hairdos were an important fashion statement. One strange hairstyle, popular with Mauryan men, had the hair tied in a knot just above the forehead. Women wore jewelled headdresses with strings of pearls framing their faces. Their hair would be plaited, knotted and curled, and covered with flowers in elaborate styles. Silk was very expensive and both silk and cotton were dyed, printed and embroidered. In winter, people wore clothes padded and quilted with cotton or wool. And they also wore pointed toed, high-heeled shoes!

Kalidasa describes make-up boxes stocked with nail cutters, perfumed pastes, scented powders, combs, curlers and a round polished piece of metal used as a mirror. There was a bottle with one end pierced like a perfume spray, and a stick of wax that looked like a lipstick. Women used henna to paint their hands and feet in delicate patterns, adorned their eyes with kohl and chewed paan to redden their lips. Cosmetics were made with flowers, spices and infusions of plants; perfumes were made from flowers, aloe and sandalwood. A dot of sindoor or vermilion was placed on the forehead, and lac turned the tip of fingers and toes a pretty pink. Sandalwood paste was used to draw pretty designs on the face, but tattoos were not known. One popular fashion of the times that has fortunately not survived is of men dying their beard in bright colours like green and purple!

Mauryan jewellery was rather chunky, but by Gupta times we see delicately crafted earrings and bangles on the sculptures. Many items were given poetic names, like kanchana kundala, tremulous earrings; vijayantika, a necklace with separate strings of pearls, rubies, emeralds and diamonds that must have cost the earth; and anklets called manjira and kinkini. Women also wore girdles at the waist and bracelets shaped like snakes for the upper arms. Jewellery for the hair was worn on top of the head, woven into hairdos, and on the forehead. They wore anklets filled with small stones that jangled as they walked. Men wore quite a lot of jewellery too, like earrings, bangles and necklaces. Surprisingly, the nose ring was not known at all.

IT'S PLAYTIME FOLKS!

People celebrated Holi, Dussehra, Deepavali and a festival to Kama, the god of love. They enjoyed plays and dance performances; bards and minstrels would sing songs and tell tales; snake charmers, acrobats, jugglers and magicians would put on their shows at market places. King Samudragupta, who was a famous warrior, was also a poet and musician, and on some of his coins he is shown playing the veena. Animal and bird fights were very popular till Ashoka banned them.

People would get very excited when a travelling theatre troupe came to town. The actors would build a wooden stage and as there was no electricity, performances were held during daytime. Women did act, though sometimes young boys played the female roles. The troupes had comedians, acrobats, dancers and a chorus of singers. The director was also the stage manager and handled the props. He was called the sutradhar, the rope holder, as he pulled up the curtain. One wonders if they had a prompter sitting in the wings!

Men were proud to be warriors, so they raced on horses and chariots, fought with swords and held archery contests. The books do not mention athletics—races or jumps—but boxing and wrestling were popular. Gambling is mentioned often in books as one of the vices of the rich young men, who wandered around gambling dens in expensive clothes, sipping wine. Obviously like the rich young people of today, it was considered the trendy thing to do.

Indians have always loved board games and there was one using counters and dice quite like ludo! One popular game was called pasaka that used three oblong dice with numbers on each side and people would bet money. It was a pasaka match that was played in the Mahabharata where Yudhishtira lost everything to Shakuni, who had loaded the dice.

Then there was a complicated game with a board of sixty-four black and white squares, two dice and pieces named king, minister, soldier, elephant, horse, camel and chariot. Sounds familiar? This was chaturanga, a game of four (chatur) armies (anga) who battled across the board for supremacy. This game of war strategy would one day evolve into chess. It is said in the Ramayana that chaturanga was invented by Ravana, the king of Lanka, to amuse his wife Mandodari and she beat him at it immediately! It was a much more complex game with four players, and their moves were decided by a throw of the dice.

An Indian king sent a chaturanga board to the king of Persia and the Persians called it 'chatranj'. The Arabs took it to Europe through the Muslim kingdoms of Spain, where it became so popular it was played in parks and public squares. Chess players can still be seen brooding over their boards in parks across Spain. Here it evolved into the chess we know today. Somewhere along the way the dice disappeared, the game became restricted to two players, the camel became the bishop and the chief minister was transformed into a powerful queen. In shatranj when one player won, he said, 'Shah maat' or the 'king is dead', as we say 'checkmate!'

The Pallavas and Cholas
(600 CE–1100 CE)

A Day in the Life of Divakar

Divakar always enjoyed polishing the bronze image of a deity—gods like Vishnu or Murugan; beautiful goddesses like Durga or Saraswati. But his favourite was the statue of Nataraja, Lord Shiva, the lord of the celestial dance. Divakar knew that one day his father would let him make his own images, but till now all he had been allowed to do was polish them.

He asked his father again, 'Appa, when will you let me make my own image?'

His father, busy carving, asked, 'Tell me how you will make it.'

'I will first carve the image in wax and then cover the wax with clay. Then I'll pour the liquid metal through a hole into the clay model and let the melted wax pour out. Once the bronze has cooled I'll break the clay and my Nataraja would be ready for polishing. Simple!'

His father looked up, 'Is it? You have to first learn what every god or goddess looks like. Their clothes, their poses, what they carry in their hands...'

Divakar was bent low over a Nataraja, carefully cleaning the rough edges and making the metal sparkle. To amuse himself he closed his eyes and tried to remember correctly what Shiva wore and held in his four hands. He wore a snake as a necklace, and the Ganga and the moon adorned his hair that flared out around his face as if he was whirling. The rear left hand held a flame and the rear right one, a drum. The front two hands were curved in a dance mudra over his bent knee, and he was dancing on top of the evil dwarf Apasmara as he was circled by an arch of flames. Divakar opened his eyes and checked... yes, he had got it right.

◆◆◆

Divakar's father is making one of the famous Chola bronze images that were made in the kingdom of Thanjavur in Tamil Nadu. They are still made the same way by an intricate system called the lost wax process.

During the time when the Mauryans and Guptas were ruling in the north, the scene in the south was often rather confusing as many dynasties rose and fell across the peninsula. There were the Chalukyas, Pallavas, Pandyas, Cholas and Cheras ruling in different parts of the Deccan region and often fighting with each other. Here we'll look at the two most illustrious southern dynasties—the Pallavas of Kanchipuram and then the Cholas of Thanjavur. Let's see what it must have been like to live during their times.

In many ways, life in villages and cities were pretty similar to that in the north, but in some matters it was quite different. The people in the south had their own language, literature and developed a rich tradition in sculpture, painting, classical music, dance and even cuisines. The southern kingdoms also became very prosperous through trade with the Roman Empire, and the kings built temples and patronized the arts, thereby evolving a rich cultural tapestry.

SINGING TO THE GODS

We get an image of life in South India from one of the greatest collection of literature in India—the ancient Sangam poetry of Tamil Nadu in the 5th and 6th century. The Sangam literature was preserved as carefully as the Rig Veda and fortunately, most of it was written down. The Sangam literature was followed by the great Bhakti poets who praised Lord Shiva and Lord Vishnu in thousands of hymns that they sang at temples. As these poets composed in Tamil instead of Sanskrit, people could understand their poetry and the hymns became very popular.

The worshippers of Vishnu were called Alvars, and of Shiva the Nayanmars. Together with magnificent poets like Sambandar, Appar, Sundarar were also poetesses like Andal and Akka Mahadevi, and even outcaste poets like Nandana and Thiruppan. Bhakti means faith, and what these poets said to people was that they are free to pray directly to their deity and do not need the services of priests. In beautiful verses they said that it did not matter whether they were rich or poor, male or female or belonged to a high caste or low. If you prayed with your heart, the gods heard you.

Unlike the Brahmins who kept people away from the rituals of worship, what these great poet-philosophers did was bring the gods closer to people. They treated all people as equals, and it started a revolution in a society that was divided by rigid caste rules. These poets began to be worshipped as saints, and their

poetry is sung in the sanctums of temples even today. The Bhakti movement slowly spread to the north where poet-thinkers like Kabir and Guru Nanak would say the same things.

THE CALL OF THE SEA

The Pallavas and Cholas ruled in the region of modern Tamil Nadu, and an important part of people's daily lives was the presence of the sea. The Pallava king Narasimha Varman was called Mahamalla or the great sailor. He built a port on the Bay of Bengal and named it Mammallapuram. From here ships carrying textiles, spices, ivory, sandalwood and precious gems sailed for the Persian Gulf and on to Europe and the far eastern lands of Cambodia, Java and Sumatra. All along the coast there were other ports like Nagapattinam, Kaveripattinam

and Arikamedu that were busy with ships and merchants. This trade thus made the people quite prosperous.

The sea gave a livelihood to the fishermen, who went out before dawn and came back as the sun rose with their boats filled with wriggling fish. The day's catch would then be taken to the nearest market town to be sold. There were divers who went searching for pearls, and it was very dangerous work as this was before we had oxygen cylinders. The boat builders of the region were famous for crafting large ships that did not use any nails; just planks of wood tied with coir ropes and these ships could stay afloat on the roughest seas.

Many men joined the merchant ships as sailors and voyaged to new lands and came back after months, even years, because sailing was a dangerous life. The ports were busy cosmopolitan places as trading ships from other countries would arrive; merchants talking in strange tongues—Arabs, Persians, Jews, Armenians, Chinese, Cambodian and Javanese—would wander around the markets. They must have had some interesting conversations!

The Pallavas and Cholas traded in goods like spices, perfumes, pottery, pearls, sandalwood and metalware, but our most famous export was textiles. Next to farmers, the largest number of people in the villages were weavers. The women and children would spin the cotton thread that would then be dyed using vegetable dyes like red safflower, indigo, madder, turmeric and vermilion. Then the men wove them into intricately patterned muslins and silks that were so delicate they were described as 'webs of woven wind', 'vapours of milk' and 'silk in a spider's web'.

Indian textiles were the best in the world and were taken to Europe and East Asia. Many of the patterns like the Indonesian batik are inspired by Indian designs. The English pattern called chinz comes from our prints called 'chhint', and the paisley is actually the mango design we call 'ambi'. The Roman ladies were very fond of Indian textiles, especially the thin, nearly transparent muslins that shocked many people. The most

...VAPOURS OF MILK, WEBS OF WOVEN WIND, SILK IN A SPIDER'S WEB...

WOW!! COOL!!

famous southern textiles were the cotton and silk brocades of Kanchipuram, kalamkari and patola from Andhra Pradesh and the ikat weaves of Orissa. We wear these fabrics even today.

CLANGING TEMPLE BELLS

In the beginning, temples were built with brick and wood, and it was the Pallavas who built some of the earliest free-standing stone temples in India. At Mamallapuram and Kanchipuram they built stone temples with walls and pillars covered with intricate carvings of gods and goddesses, demons and celestial maidens, and this began our great tradition of stone sculpture. Stone carving became a hereditary art where fathers taught their sons. Even today the workshops of stone carvers are alive and filled with the sound of chisels and hammers in Mamallapuram, north of Chennai.

The kings built their palaces in wood and brick, but their temples were made of lasting stone. So the palaces may have vanished but the temples still stand proud. Every dynasty built temples in its capital city, and Pallava temples can be seen at Kanchipuram while the Chalukyan shrines are at Badami. The most famous Pandyan creation is the Meenakshi Temple at Madurai, and the Brihadishwara Temple in Thanjavur is the greatest creation of the Chola king Raja Raja I.

Temples became the heart of new towns and cities that grew around them. These temples became the centre of not just religion but also trade, art and culture. A southern temple is a world of its own, and even today in the temple towns of the south the tall gopuram gateways pierce the skyline and the lives of the people are deeply influenced by the great shrines and the pilgrims who visit them. Like they have done for two thousand years, these temples still provide a livelihood to flower and fruit sellers, craftsmen, cooks, tourist guides, priests, astrologers and innkeepers.

Today if you wander into a temple complex in Chidambaram, Srirangam, Kanchipuram or Rameswaram, you can still get an idea of what they were like over a thousand years ago. You walk in under the high gopuram gateway and then enter the first of many courtyards that have the mandapams, open-pillared hallways that are used by pilgrims. Then the entrance to the next courtyard will also be through a gopuram, and then in the heart of the complex will be the main shrines of the god and his consort.

The image of the deity always stands in the sanctum called the garbha griha, adorned with flowers, silks and jewels, wreathed in incense smoke and lit by tall earthen lamps. Here worshippers make their offerings as the priests intone mantras. This is where the main daily religious ceremonies are held—the arati when a many-flamed lamp is waved before the deity; in the past, the devadasis danced to the beat of drums and flutes, and singers sang hymns. These temples became a part of the daily life of the people who went for the daily pujas, attended cultural gatherings and joined the processions during festivals.

The main street of the town led off from the temple gateway and it was lined by shops and inns. Here shops sold what pilgrims needed for their worship—flower garlands, incense, fruits, sweets, images, bowls and plates. Then there were food shops, weavers selling textiles, jewellers and spice merchants. Kings donated villages to these temples and the income from these villages was used to run them. Important temples employed hundreds of people—not just priests but garland makers, dancers, singers, accountants, stone carvers, carpenters, cleaners and guards.

A CULTURED WORLD

The arts and crafts patronized by these temples are being practised even today. The weavers of Kanchipuram are still creating magic with their looms, and the beautiful Chola bronze images are still made in Thanjavur. We have all seen the famous image of the dancing Nataraja with his hair flaring out around his head. That is a classic Chola bronze sculpture, and these images are made today at Swamimalai using exactly the same process as two thousand years ago.

The temples also became centres of culture with dancers, singers and poets gathering from across the kingdom. They provided regular work to stone carvers and mural painters as the royalty and nobility built more temples, till a pilgrim town would have a dozen shrines. This was also the time when forms of dances like the Bharatanatyam and Kuchipudi, and the traditions of classical Carnatic music, were laid by temple dancers called devadasis and their musicians. In the Thanjavur temple, there is a hall where all the Bharatanatyam postures are carved on the wall like a dance lesson written in stone. If today we have such a proud tradition of classical music and dance, such a dazzling variety of woven cottons and silks, stone and metal crafts, it is because they were nurtured at these temples.

ALWAYS READY FOR APPAMS!

In India we take our food very seriously. Imagine the appam being mentioned in a book, *Perumpanuru*, in the 5th century CE and poets singing the praises of the dosai in 6th century Tamil Sangam literature! Today we have food shops frying dosas in every city, and Kerala restaurants serve appams, those delicious rice pancakes, with meen (fish) curry and Kerala stew.

The daily life of the people was pretty similar to that of people in the north. Clothes were the same, though in the south, as the weather was warmer, men often wore only the lower garment and preferred to adorn themselves with necklaces and bangles. It was the food that was cooked differently because there were different varieties of vegetables, spices and fruits available. For example, recipes used more of tamarind, curry leaves and coconut. And there was the aroma of the many spices grown in Kerala like pepper, cardamom, cloves and nutmeg. Traders

came from across the world to buy them and Indian spices were so precious in Europe, they were paid for in gold!

Rice, which was the main cereal, was cooked in many delicious ways—as pancakes called appams, the fried dosais, and sweetened with coconut milk as idiappams. Interestingly, the idli was not made in the early centuries of the first millennium; at least it was not mentioned in the books. Being near the sea they ate more fish, crabs and prawns and the Tamil word for fish 'meen' soon entered the Sanskrit language. Cane and palm sugar were used for sweets, and people enjoyed a delicious drink called munnir made of sugar cane juice, coconut water and palm sugar.

The Deccan peninsula is huge, and slowly various regions developed their own styles of cooking. The four main ones that we know today are that of Andhra, Karnataka, Tamil Nadu and Kerala. Books often talk of feasts and the overeating of the greedy guest, describing a man who ate so much he burst the waist strings of his dhoti and could not get up!

The rich also enjoyed the foodstuffs that arrived by ship, like Italian wine! Many Roman gold coins and two-handled amphorae have been found along the coast. We also read in the books about ladies of Tamil noble families, all dressed up in silks, gold jewellery and jasmine garlands, having a great time sipping wine at parties.

Three: MEDIEVAL INDIA

The Delhi Sultanate
The Mughals

THE DELHI SULTANATE
(1200 CE–1500 CE)

A DAY IN THE LIFE OF SALIM

As the sun set, the pilgrims began to gather before the marble pillared pavilion. The oil lamps were being lit all around the shrine of the Sufi saint Sheikh Nizamuddin Auliya of Delhi, the air redolent with the perfume of flowers and incense.

This day was very special for Salim. Tonight, for the first time in his life, he was going to sing here before hundreds of people. He cleared his throat and tried to focus on the music. His father was a famous qawwali singer, and his team was going to perform at the shrine today. The sarangi player was tuning his instrument, the tabla player tapping at the knots of his tabla, and Salim sat in the chorus, ready to clap and sing.

Salim felt his heart begin to thud with nervousness. He had not felt like this, he thought puzzled, when they were rehearsing at home. That morning he had sung so well that even his strict

Abbu had given a small nod of approval. Why was his mouth dry now, and his ears filled with this strange humming noise? Just then Adil, his older brother who played the sarangi, turned to him and gave a quick smile. 'Getting nervous are we?'

'Ummm yes . . . a little . . .'

Adil pointed to the marble shrine before him. 'Who is buried there?'

'Sheikh Nizamuddin.'

'He was the kindest man on the face of earth. Whatever you sing, if you sing with your heart, he will understand.'

'Ji Bhaiya.'

Salim murmured a quick prayer to the kind saint, and to his relief his heart stopped thudding. Then his father's deep, clear baritone rose in the air as he began a famous qawwali composed by Amir Khusro, who was Sheikh Nizamuddin's favourite disciple. Salim closed his eyes, gently swaying to the lovely melody and then softly, he raised his voice and joined in.

◆ ◆ ◆

Salim, singing to a Sufi saint, must have lived in 14th century Delhi, and it is possible that his grandfather had come to India from Afghanistan.

North India faced a social upheaval in the last years of the 12th century when for the first time a Muslim dynasty began to rule in Delhi. With a sultan on the throne, there was a huge influx of people from Afghanistan, Persia, Arabia and Turkey, who came seeking work and eventually settled in India.

This meant that Indians now came into contact with a new religion, Islam, and as it was the first religion that did not start

in India, it was very different. Also, the new people brought with them their own social customs, food and clothing, that were new to Hindu society. Both sides influenced each other and interestingly, what came out of it was a civilization of great variety and colour that was uniquely Indian.

People living in the ports of the western coast, in Kerala and Gujarat, were already familiar with Muslim culture as many Arab traders had settled there. The kings had allowed them to practise their religion and many of them married Indian women, like those belonging to the Moplah community of Kerala who were originally Arabs. These traders had no ambition of conquering the land, becoming kings or spreading their religion and so lived amicably among the seaside population.

Then Muslim invaders like Mahmud of Ghazni swept into India, looted the temples and went away. But Muhammad of Ghur came to stay. His rule was followed by other dynasties like the Mamluks, Khiljis, Tughlaqs, Sayyids and Lodis. They together comprised the Delhi Sultanate. The Delhi Sultans conquered North India, and there was a steady migration of men from Muslim countries seeking a career in the new kingdom. Then as the Delhi Sultanate began to decline, new kingdoms rose in the Deccan, like Golconda, Bijapur, Ahmednagar, Bidar, and Berar and these are called the Deccan Sultanates. By the 14th century, the only Hindu kingdom to survive in the Deccan was Vijayanagar that defied the Deccan Sultanates for over two centuries.

We get a portrait of the life of the people of this period in the writings of royal historians like Amir Khusro and Ziauddin Barani. Many travellers like the Persian Al Biruni, Ibn Batuta from Morocco, the Portuguese Domingo Paes and the Italian Nicolo Conti also wrote about this. They have left behind fascinating accounts of their adventures in India.

LET'S BUILD A CITY

The towns and cities looked rather different from today, as they were much smaller, with fewer people. The roads were dusty and bumpy, made of flattened earth, and sometimes paved with cobblestones. On it moved the traffic of horses, palanquins, bullock carts, camels and an elephant or two. It was also very noisy with the rattle of wooden cart wheels, the clatter of horses' hooves and the shouts of drivers. Most people just walked as there was no system of public transport.

There was also no system of city planning. Usually the sultan built his fortress surrounded by a high stone wall and the city would grow around it in a completely haphazard manner. The fortress had his palaces and offices. A broad avenue led off from the main gateway, and it had shops on both sides with the shopkeepers living above their shops. These were brick buildings, whitewashed, with a simple square design covered with a flat roof. Then there were narrow, serpentine

OVER SPEEDING!!

lanes curving away from the main avenue with random clusters of mansions, huts and workshops.

The rich lived in large whitewashed brick mansions that were hidden behind high walls and had gardens, ponds and wells. The poor only had single-roomed thatched huts and maybe an attached room where the craftsmen worked at their looms, potter's wheel or carpenter's stand. There was no regular system of garbage collection or underground drainage, so the streets were pretty smelly as dirty water poured down open drains and garbage collected in corners.

As the houses were built very close together in narrow lanes, these towns became fire traps, and every summer fires would rage through them. There was no fire brigade of course, so entire rows of houses would turn to ashes. Of course cities of this time across the world were similar sights. The cities were surrounded by a broad protective stone and rubble boundary wall pierced by tall gateways that was guarded by soldiers. The gates were closed at dusk and soldiers marched along the top of the wall all night.

People from nearby towns and villages came to shop at the bazaars. One bazaar is described by Francois Bernier during the reign of Shahjahan in the 17th century: 'For one that makes a display of beautiful and fine cloths, silk, and other stuffs striped with gold and silver, turbans embroidered with gold

HOW MUCH ARE THESE FOR? OOOOPS...

and brocades, there are at least five and twenty where nothing is seen but pots of oil and butter, piles of baskets filled with rice, barley, chickpeas and wheat.'

Vendors wandered through the streets, calling out their wares and selling vegetables, clothes, pottery and metalware. Shops and houses were lighted by oil lamps, as candles would come into use only by Mughal times, and the cooking was done on smoky wood chullahs. Sometimes lanes were completely enveloped by the smoke from these chullahs which made people cough. Markets had food shops and caravanserais where men sat gossiping over glasses of sherbet and wine. In fact by the time of Jahangir, Delhi and Agra even had a few fashionable coffee shops.

YEH DILLI HAI!

The character of the cities changed as power shifted to Muslims, and Hindus were no longer allowed to hold high office. It now rested with three new social groups—the king, the nobility,

who were also the army generals, and the religious leaders
called the Ulema, who gave judgements according to the Quran.
The streets began to look different, as people from Muslim
countries wandered around in their strange clothes, speaking
in strange languages.

The rich were either the Muslim nobility or the Hindu
merchants who lived in huge mansions with gardens, ponds
and stables for horses and elephants. Then there were the men
who worked in the offices of the government, the clerks who sat
on cushions on the floor with low tables before them, with the
official papers kept in rolls on wall shelves. The poor worked
as servants, washer men, gardeners, cooks, stable hands and
soldiers, and they were all paid measly sums. So very often the
women in poor families also had to go out to work.

Slavery was common, and the rich owned a large number of
slaves. However, unlike Europe where slaves were used in
agriculture and mines, here they usually worked in homes. Sultan
Firuz Shah Tughlaq is said to have owned two lakh slaves. Slavery,
however, was not a rigid system and many able slaves gained
their freedom and became officials and army commanders. The
most famous example is Qutubuddin Aibak, who was a slave
of Muhammad of Ghur and became the sultan of Delhi at his
master's death. Aibak's slave Balban also became Sultan, and so
this dynasty is called the Mamluk or the Slave Dynasty. Alauddin
Khilji's favourite slave Malik Kafur led military expeditions to
the south, became fabulously rich and at the death of his master
even tried to set up a puppet sultan on the throne.

There were some professions we have not known earlier, like
bhishtis who brought fresh drinking water from the river in huge
leather bags. There were lamplighters too, who came out at dusk
to light the torches at the corners of the streets. As there were
no printing presses, calligraphers copied out books by hand and
they were very expensive. Rich people had special rooms where
these manuscripts were carefully stored on shelves. The rich

had large stables where stable hands and horse trainers were employed. There were men to pull the fans called pankhas. The horse carriage driver, elephant mahout and palanquin bearers have been replaced by bus and taxi drivers today.

PRAYERS AT DAWN

Mosques came up in the cities and Hindus were not allowed to build new temples, but could preserve the old ones. Hindus were called zimmis, or people who followed a different faith, and had to pay the jiziya tax that allowed them to practise their own religion. As the majority of the people were Hindus, the religion survived; but Buddhism vanished from the land of its birth and you no longer saw the saffron-clad monks on their morning begging rounds. The Buddhist monasteries at Taxila and Sarnath were destroyed by the sultans, and the greatest tragedy was the burning of the University of Nalanda and its legendary collection of manuscripts. All this led to a period of darkness in academics as the Brahmin scholars became fearful and hid their books, while the Buddhist scholars were gone. There was little progress in literature, science or mathematics during this period, and India began to fall behind Europe.

There were two streams of religious thought that became very popular among the common people, and both played a role in building bridges between the Hindus and the Muslims. One was the Sufi tradition among the Muslims and the other, the Bhakti movement among the Hindus. Both the faiths were humane, tolerant and welcomed people of every caste, creed and colour. The shrines of Sufi saints like Muinuddin Chishti at Ajmer, or Sheikh Nizamuddin Auliya at Delhi, were open to all and no one asked the religion of a pilgrim.

Similarly, poet-thinkers like Kabir and Guru Nanak preached a love of humanity and equality. They were the voice of the people, and for them god was a wise guide and friend. They preached that you did not need Brahmin priests or Muslim mullahs to gain his blessings. For the great weaver-poet Kabir everyone was equal, all religions were the same and there was only one god.

Kabir wrote in one of his short dohas, translated here by another humanist poet, Rabindranath Tagore:

> Hari is in the East; Allah is in the west.
> Look within your heart, for there you will find both Karim and Ram.
> All the men and women of the world are His living forms,
> Kabir is the child of Allah and of Ram. He is my Guru, he is my Pir.

The Sufi and Bhakti faiths became popular in the Sultanate period and played a vital role in building tolerance and understanding among the various religious communities. When a Muslim and a Hindu sat together and listened to the songs of Guru Nanak or swayed to the qawwalis at a dargah, they forgot their mutual suspicions and became just human beings. It also led to the priests of the two main faiths of Hinduism and Islam to change their ways and not foment intolerance and hatred because they sensed that people did not welcome it.

A NEW WAY OF LIVING

Earlier, society used to be strictly divided along caste and religious lines, and Hindus and Muslims stayed socially apart. But now, many Hindus converted to Islam because it helped them in getting jobs in the government. Some lower castes too chose to convert as a way to escape their miserable lives. As Hindus and Muslims began to live side by side, they gradually began to influence each other in many subtle ways. What India is today, which is a wonderfully colourful melting pot of many cultures, began at this time of synthesis that enriched our lives.

Every aspect of people's lives—social habits, religious practices, clothes, cuisine, education, art and literature—was touched by change and in many ways the arrival of a new, young, vigorous culture was a positive thing for Indian life. For example, we got some great writers and historians, musicians and artists, craftsmen and chefs, all making our lives more vibrant and interesting. What emerged in a few centuries, by the time of the Mughals, was uniquely Indian.

BORN A GIRL

The life of women was never easy, and with the Muslims came the tradition of the harem and purdah that made matters worse. Rich Muslim families kept their women in seclusion in a guarded section of the house, where they were not allowed to meet any man who did not belong to the family. Even when these women went out, they were covered in the burqua and had to be accompanied by men. The penalty for breaking the purdah was severe. The English traveller Edward Terry writes about the wife of a nobleman, who jumped from the howdah of a maddened elephant to save herself and thus revealed her face. Her husband divorced her immediately as she had supposedly brought shame to the family!

Polygamy or marrying many wives was common among both Hindus and Muslims. Hindu widows were not allowed to remarry. The worst was the growing incidents of sati, where Hindu widows were burnt on the funeral pyre of their husbands. This was very common among rich families and was usually done so that the dead man's property could be grabbed by the family.

SCHOOL? NO WAY!

Most people did not go to school and people learnt just enough to be able to do their work. For example, the son of a merchant would learn to do the calculations and write simple letters. Girls were not educated at all. Most of the teachers were priests—the Brahmins for the Hindus and the Maulvis for the Muslims. The Islamic primary schools, called maktabs, were attached to mosques, and the Brahmins taught at schools called pathshalas or tol. Most of the teachers were not very well educated themselves and taught a mishmash of reading and writing of Sanskrit, Persian or Arabic, a smattering of arithmetic and always, the very boring memorizing of religious books.

It was no fun going to school as the boys spent hours and hours bent over the books, swaying and repeating the words. If they got bored and stopped, the teacher's stick would land on their back with a whack. So most boys stopped going to school and only a few went to colleges. Apparently some courses lasted for sixteen years! The Hindu colleges were called gurukuls and the Muslim students went to madrasas. Many gurukuls were found in holy cities like Varanasi and Madurai. A madrasa in Multan was famous for astronomy and mathematics, and one in Sirhind trained students in Ayurveda and Unani medicines.

Colleges were established by rich people and they taught subjects like law, medicine and astronomy. Boys who wanted to become priests studied astrology, grammar, logic and theology, while literature and history were chosen by boys planning to join the bureaucracy. Notice, there was no science or geography in the curriculum! And that odd interest in logic was very mysterious. What could you do with your life after spending ten years studying the art of logical argument?

KEBABS ARE HERE!

With the arrival of Muslims, the most delicious changes took place in Indian cooking. Muslims introduced a cuisine that used baking and the tandoori ovens. They brought with them many varieties of breads and a wide range of roasted meat dishes. Indian cooks now synthesized the two styles and produced some classic dishes.

Take breads—the Hindus had the puri which is a round piece of dough fried in ghee, and the Muslims had dry baked breads called khameeri roti. Now the Muslim bread, first baked lightly on a tawa, was then sautéed in ghee like a puri and you got the delectable parantha! Yum!

Indian spices were a revelation to the Muslim chefs, and the
kebab platter grew. Meat was now cooked in gravy in kormas
and kalias. Muslim baking techniques were used to create new
rice dishes like the pulaos and biryanis. Then desserts got more
interesting. Hindus had the kheer and payasam; now the rice
was ground and mixed in cream and we had the phirni. The
halwa arrived from Turkey, the jalebi from Arabia and barfis
and laddus were now enriched with dried fruits like almonds,
walnuts and raisins from Afghanistan.

Everyone chewed paan, and there were paan shops everywhere.
Tobacco was brought to India by the Portuguese during the
reign of Jahangir (while coffee was brought by the Arabs). Tea
was also known, but people did not drink tea or coffee at home
as they were considered to be intoxicants. For a while coffee
became the fashionable drink of the rich, and there were coffee
shops in Delhi and Agra where men sat sipping from small cups
and gossiping, pretty much like what we do today.

THE MUGHALS
(1550 CE–1850 CE)

A DAY IN THE LIFE OF SHAHEEN

Shaheen and her mother spread out the length of silk. It was the colour of new grass, a soft shade of emerald, and on it they were embroidering a pattern of curving flowers and leaves. Shaheen carefully threaded the golden silk into her needle and began to make tiny stitches along the pattern that her mother had drawn on the cloth.

This design had to be perfect, Shaheen thought. This silk was to be used as a chunari by a nobleman's daughter, who was getting married the next week. Shaheen and her mother would work all day and then late into the night by the light of an oil lamp to finish it on time. Sometimes her eyes ached and watered as she worked, but they were being paid well for this work. As she worked, Shaheen dreamed that may be one day she would earn enough to buy a piece of silk for a blouse.

'I want blue...with silver work...not gold,' Shaheen said dreamily.

Her mother raised her head, 'Blue what?'

'A blue silk blouse embroidered in silver thread.'

'I could embroider a blue cotton blouse for you,' her mother said gently. 'It would be just as pretty. Silk is very expensive, beti.' Then her mother looked thoughtful and said, 'There is something we can do.' Shaheen sat up, her eyes shining. 'Go get that bundle from the clothes box,' her mother ordered.

Shaheen ran to get the bundle which was full of odd bits and pieces of cloth left over from the clothes her father stitched. He was a tailor. They found two large pieces of silk, one blue, the other purple and her mother said, 'How about a blue blouse with purple sleeves?'

'Oh yes!' Shaheen smiled widely. 'And I'll do the embroidery!'

◆ ◆ ◆

With the arrival of Zahiruddin Babur began the vibrantly colourful and endlessly entertaining reign of the Mughals that made the dynasty a legend across the world. For two centuries they were the epitome of grandeur and power, while the first six kings—Babur, Humayun, Akbar, Jahangir, Shahjahan and Aurangzeb—were truly great monarchs. Akbar laid the foundations of the Mughal Empire that covered nearly the whole of the Indian subcontinent and went up to Kabul in Afghanistan. The stories of this legendary empire of the 'Mogols' brought travellers, artists, missionaries and adventurers from across the world to Agra and Delhi.

There is such a wide range of writings on the Mughal royal histories, memoirs of Jesuits, books of travellers, and so on— that one is spoilt for choice. From the multi-volume history of Akbar's reign, the *Ain-i-Akbari* and *Akbarnama* by Abul Fazl, to the royal chronicle of the *Badshahnama* about Shahjahan and the writings of European travellers like Manucci, Francois Bernier, Jean Baptiste Tavernier, Ralph Fitch et al. and the Jesuits Fr. Monserrate and Aquaviva—we get everything from official histories to personal memoirs and bazaar gossip. There is also a lot of visual information about clothes and jewellery, furniture and furnishing that can be found in the rich hoard of Mughal miniature paintings.

There was a lot that did not change from the time of the Sultanate, like the daily lives of people. What fascinated the world was the glamorous lives of the Mughals. They were like the film stars of today, with people exchanging gossip about their lives.

RICH MAN, POOR MAN

There was a stark contrast between the lives of the poor and the noblemen, who lived in extravagant luxury. The poor lived in huddles of thatched huts, usually one windowless room, walls of bare brick, the floor made of earth spread with pounded cow dung, and a small courtyard where they would keep cows or buffaloes. They had few possessions, no furniture, and slept on mats or string cots and even under the sky during summer. Their kitchens had mainly earthen pots, and most people had only a few sets of clothes. The streets were dirty as they had no drainage system and there were only a few wells for water.

The homes of the rich were hidden behind high walls and divided into two sections—the outer area for the men called the mardana, and the inner was for women called the zenana. These mansions, called havelis, had rooms around many interconnected courtyards, ponds, gardens with fountains, kitchens, stables and servant's quarters. The sitting room or diwan khana was furnished with expensive carpets on which large bolsters were placed, as people preferred to sit on the

floor or on low diwans. There were a few low stools too, but no chairs. Candleholders and oil lamps were made of brass or glass, and the rooms were perfumed by burning incense. In summer, servants stood behind the people, waving large fans. There were larger fans made of long lengths of cloth attached to the ceiling, called pankhas, that were pulled with a rope by a servant. Often the punkhawalla would tie the rope to his big toe and relax and smoke a hookah.

The rich travelled in palanquins called palki, doli or dola, carried by two, four or even eight men called kahars. The larger, more luxurious palkis had cushioned seats and could carry up to three persons. Women travelled in covered horse carriages and palkis. The royal women often rode on elephant back in covered howdahs. The poor, of course, walked or took a ride on the back of a buffalo.

MUGHAL SPLENDOUR

The life of the Mughal royal family fascinated people because a Mughal palace was a unique world of its own. It was the third Mughal king, Akbar, who began the tradition of building fortresses with many palaces inside. He built them at Agra, Allahabad and Lahore, and then built a whole new city at Fatehpur Sikri. However, the finest Mughal fortress was built by his grandson Shahjahan at Delhi, the citadel we call the Red Fort.

Shahjahan named it the Qila-i-Maula or the Fortunate Fortress, and it saw the most extravagant and luxurious lifestyle in the world. Behind high red sandstone walls was a whole world of public and private palaces, offices, gardens, water pools, stables, kitchens and the quarters of slaves, servants and soldiers. People entered through the Lahori Darwaza gate into the Chhatta Chowk, a bazaar, and then reached the Naubat Khana or Drum House where the imperial drums boomed out to announce the time or to welcome important guests. This led to a pavilion called the Diwan-i-Am or the Hall of Public Audiences, and here Shahjahan sat on a silver throne wearing silks and jewels and held court.

From early morning people streamed in to stand in a courtyard before the Diwan-i-Am, and there was a strict system of who stood where. The royal princes, ministers and noblemen stood closest to the king. The poorest stood right at the back behind a stone railing; the second grade nobles behind a silver railing; and right before the king's seat was a solid gold divider. There is a miniature painting showing Prince Aurangzeb opening the gate of the gold railing and entering the first enclosure as he bows deeply to his father.

Twice a day, Shahjahan arrived to the roll of drums as a crier called out his name. The crier would bestow many grand titles on the emperor as everyone bowed low. People had to remain standing and never raise their eyes to look directly at him. As the prime minister or vazir called out their names, people would go up to present their petitions, first doing the kornish—touching their right hand to their forehead and bowing low. The vazir then handed the papers to the king, listened to his orders and announced them to the waiting people.

Shahjahan worked very hard as every day there were hundreds of people coming from all across the empire to meet him; his court would go on for hours. At times the king would take a break to listen to singers or watch acrobats or dancers. Often Prince Dara Shikoh, who was his favourite, would help him with his administrative work.

Miniature paintings show Shahjahan wearing rich silks beautifully embroidered in gold. He would don a high turban, and as he loved precious gems, he glitters with jewellery—a pearl necklace set with rubies and sapphires, rings on every finger including the thumb, gold and diamond bracelets,

armlets on the upper arm and pearl earrings. His turban had a sarpech, a jewelled brooch with high feathers. Even the dagger tucked into his belt had a gold hilt set with emeralds and diamonds. With the noblemen also clad in their finest, it was a dazzling gathering.

The Diwan-i-Am was the last palace where the public was allowed to enter; and beyond it was the private world of the Mughals—a series of palaces set in delightful gardens where the royal family stayed. One had to enter through a small gate that was guarded by soldiers. A red curtain used to hang across this gate and so it was called Lal Purdah Darwaza. It was, in fact, such a great privilege to be allowed in that the lucky people who could go in were called Lal Purdaris.

Right in front were the rows of elegant marble palaces at one end of green lawns. To the right was the Mughal harem or zenana. In Mughal times, these palaces were hidden behind high hedges and guarded by soldiers. Three harem palaces— Chhoti Baithak, Mumtaz Mahal and Rang Mahal—stood in a row, and through them a stream of water flowed along a carved marble channel with fountains to cool the rooms. This stream was called Nahr-i-Bihisht or the stream of paradise. Chhoti Baithak has disappeared, so the first palace on the extreme right is the Mumtaz Mahal, where Princess Jahanara used to stay. Now it is a museum.

Next was Rang Mahal where the senior queens lived, built all in marble with delicately carved pillars and ceiling. The Nahr-i-Bihisht flowed down the rooms along a marble channel with a lotus-shaped fountain in the middle. The fountain had a coloured inlay of flowers around it. When water flowed over it, the petals danced and swayed as if they had come alive.

A row of screened windows faced the river Jamuna, flowing right below the walls of the fort. The women lived in great luxury, relaxing on plush carpets, leaning against bolsters, as the fountain splashed and the sunlight sparkled on the gold ceiling. There were two corner rooms called Sheesh Mahal, with mirrors set in the ceilings and walls. Here at night, as maids went past carrying lamps, the light would be reflected in the hundreds of tiny mirrors, and the golden flames of candles would dance into the night.

The Khas Mahal was the personal palace of Shahjahan, and his private apartments were sumptuously decorated. His bedroom was called Khwabgah, or the chamber of dreams; the Tosh Khana was his dressing room; the Baithak was the sitting room and there was a prayer room called the Tasbih Khana, or the chamber for telling one's beads. Near the ceiling was a delicately carved marble screen with the scale of justice. Facing the river was the balcony called Mussaman Burj, where Shah

Jahan appeared every morning to show himself to his subjects gathered below. This ceremony, called Jharokha-i-Darshan, reassured the people that he was alive and all was well with the empire.

Now we come to the Diwan-i-Khas, the Hall of Private Audience, where Shahjahan sat on the famous Peacock Throne. This was the stage where the Great Mughal played emperor of the richest empire in the world in magnificent grandeur. Only the most powerful men were allowed here for important work of the state. The marble walls and pillars were inlaid with designs of flowers—lilies, chrysanthemums, marigolds and curving vines and clouds, all in precious stones like agate, pearls, lapis lazuli, jade, rose quartz, jasper, onyx, turquoise and beryl. Today we wear these gems in jewellery and they cost the earth. Imagine, how rich Shahjahan was to have them inlaid on his walls! Moreover, the ceiling of this hall was covered with dazzling patterns in real gold and silver paint.

The Peacock Throne was not a chair but a diwan with pillars holding up a canopy on top, all made of solid gold and set with precious gems. A French jeweller Jean Baptiste Tavernier saw it and counted 108 rubies, 116 emeralds and several diamonds! On top of the canopy were two golden peacocks, their tails set with blue sapphires and a ruby set at their breasts with a large pearl drop. The diamond Kohinoor or the 'mountain of light' was set in front, and the edge of the canopy was hung with strings of pearls.

It must have been a magnificent scene, with the sunlight falling on the marble walls, making the inlay flowers glow and the gold ceiling dazzle. Incense smoke perfumed the air as the cool breezes flowed in from the river through the lattice screened windows. Here on a wall, this Persian couplet was inscribed, '*Agar firdaus baru-i-zamin ast. Hamin ast, hamin ast, hamin ast.*' It means, if there be a paradise of bliss on earth. It is this! It is this! It is this!

The garden in front of these palaces was called the Hayat Baksh Bagh, the Life Bestowing Garden. There was also the Mehtab Bagh, or Moonlight Garden, that was later destroyed by the British army by building very ugly barracks over it. Babur had started the tradition of building landscaped gardens, and they were laid out in straight lines with square flower beds, channels of water and rows of spurting fountains. The royal family had two garden pavilions, called Sawan and Bhadon after the monsoon months, where they enjoyed the rains. At dusk, candles were placed in niches behind water cascades to add dancing lights and shadows.

At one end of the garden were the Hammams or the royal baths, and they are the most luxurious baths you can imagine! The marble rooms had floors inlaid in floral and geometric designs, with fountains set in the centre that spurted perfumed water. There was a hot water pool and also a basin that had perfumed rose water bubbling up. Shahjahan would have his most private discussions here with his ministers as he soaked in a pool perfumed with the attar of roses!

Despite the luxury, the Mughals remained austere in their prayers. Shahjahan used to go in procession to pray at the Jama Masjid that stands on a hillock at one end of Chandni Chowk. His son Aurangzeb disliked pomp and built the marble Moti Masjid inside the fort, where he and the royal women prayed in private.

BEGUMS OF THE MAHAL

The lives of the women of the Mughal harem fascinated travellers and common people alike. The harem palaces were called the Mahal, and they were closely guarded by soldiers. All the servants here were either women or eunuch slaves. The queens, princesses and concubines lived in great luxury but no freedom. They all had their separate apartments and maids, there were gardens and water pools, regular entertainment and trips outside in covered carts, but they could not meet anyone without the permission of the king. They were like exotic birds in cages.

The most powerful women belonged to the immediate family, like the queens or princesses, who were trusted advisers of the king. Many of them, like Akbar's mother Hamida Banu Begum, or Jahangir's favourite queen, Nurjahan, read all the official papers and even attended public audiences, sitting concealed behind a screen. So they were well informed about the work of the empire. They received generous allowances and Akbar's queen Mariam-us-Zamani, popularly known as Jodh Bai, was a pretty smart lady who owned ships and traded with Europe.

Jahanara, who was a scholar and poetess, managed Shahjahan's harem and enjoyed the title of Begum Sahib as she sat on a throne to listen to the petitions. She also held the signet ring used to stamp royal orders called firmans. And you can't beat the birthday present that Shahjahan once gave to Jahanara: it was the port of Surat given for her 'expenses on paan'!

Still it was not an easy life. Akbar decreed that Mughal princesses were not to marry, in order to avoid having sons-in-law who could claim the throne. It was Aurangzeb who later changed the rule and got his daughters married. For most of the women, life was of unending idleness and luxurious boredom. They spent their days stitching, playing cards, busy with gossip and intrigue, and the only purpose of their lives was to somehow have a son which would give them more status and power. For all the curiosity they aroused, the harem was often a place of loneliness and sadness for these women.

MUGHLAI MASALA

The Mughals were gourmets who took a lot of interest in food, and today the spicy North Indian cooking is often called Mughlai cuisine. Shahjahan would sit down to a meal of at least fifty dishes made in the many kitchens inside the fort! The food arrived in sealed packets and was first tasted by the royal taster for poisons. They really worried about being poisoned and hence used jade bowls, believing that jade changes colour if the food was poisoned.

Among the new creations were many Indian breads and a growing platter of rice and meat dishes. As you will notice, vegetables were not that important to the Mughals. Among the breads, the first was the parantha, and it became so popular that a lane in Delhi's Chandni Chowk was named Paranthewali Gali! Next came the rumali or 'handkerchief' bread, where the chef throws a circle of dough up into the air with a twist of the wrist and the paper-thin roti is baked on an upturned karhai. We got the bakarkhwani from Hyderabad, which is baked bread topped with almonds, raisins and sunflower seeds. From Lucknow came the sheermal, with the dough kneaded in milk and ghee and baked with a coating of saffron, and the varqi and jalebi paranthas dripping with ghee.

The kebab was always the star of the Mughlai menu. They were deep-fried as shami kebabs or grilled on skewers like sheekh kebabs. Hyderabad gave us the shikampuri kebab with a stuffing of egg. The most famous was Lucknow's kakori kebab, crisp on the outside and creamy soft inside, which is extremely difficult to make. Legends say it was created for an old and toothless nawab!

Among the rice dishes, Delhi delighted in the menu of biryanis where rice was layered with meat or chicken and steamed with spices, ghee and saffron. Lucknow preferred the lighter pulaos cooked in handis. People of these two cities still argue which is the classier dish. The Dilliwallas say the pulao is too bland and the Lucknow gourmets think the biryani is too rich. The best solution is to taste both!

The kitchens of the rich were huge establishments with a hierarchy of chefs who specialized in cooking in different vessels. The bawarchis used large pots called degchis, while the raqabdars, who considered themselves culinary artists, used small handis and made highly complicated dishes. They had an army of kitchen assistants like the masalchis who ground masalas, the men who chopped vegetables, the assistant chefs who cut meat and fish, and so on; at the bottom were the degshors who spent all day washing the pots and pans. In Hindu vegetarian kitchens, the cook was usually a Brahmin and was respectfully called maharaj, the king of the kitchen.

MUGHAL FASHIONS

Hindu men wore cotton dhotis and kurtas and tied a turban on their head. Women wore saris with a short-sleeved blouse called angiya or choli, or lehnga skirts with blouses and a chunari covering their heads. Common people could not afford silk or wool which was very expensive, and in winter used quilted cotton jackets and caps. Every region had its speciality in textiles. In Rajasthan, there were the tie and dye fabrics called bandhni and lehriya; Gujarat produced the intricate weaves of jamawar; Varanasi was legendary for its kinkhab brocades, and it was said that the muslins woven by the weavers of Dhaka were so fine they could be passed through a ring.

The Muslim men dressed in loose pyjamas called salwars or tight churidars, and a kurta with a long coat on top called the qaba. On formal occasions they tied a scarf around their waist like a belt, called a kamarbandh or patka, and tucked a small decorative dagger in it. Muslim women also wore salwars, churidars and kurtas called angrakhas, often made of sheer, nearly transparent silk, and wore an angiya under it. Of course when they went out it was all hidden under an enveloping burqua!

The Muslim style of tying a turban was flat and round, and their turbans were usually white. The Hindus, on the other hand,

used brighter colours and tied it high and pointed. The Mughal kings enjoyed setting the fashions, and Akbar got at least two hundred sets of clothes stitched every year, many given as gifts to guests. It must have taken an army of tailors as all the stitching was done by hand. Once, the Portuguese ambassador presented sets of cloaks and jackets to Akbar and he and his two grandsons strutted around Fatehpur Sikri dressed like European grandees.

The poor usually moved around bare feet and Hindus only wore wooden slippers inside the house. Leather shoes were made in the Persian style with low heels and pointed and curling toes; only soldiers wore riding boots. The shoes were often embroidered in silk and gold thread and even set with precious stones, but shoes with laces or high heels were not known.

There were many kinds of hair oils, soaps and perfumed powders, even false hair, hair dye and fantastic cures for baldness. The bathing soap was called ghasul and was made of natural oils and perfumes. Many kinds of attar and sandalwood powder were used as perfume, and Nurjahan's mother is said to have created the attar of roses. Women darkened their eyes with kajal or kohl and silver antimony, and chewed paan to redden their lips. Henna and lac were used to decorate the hands and feet. One strange fashion was a powder called missia that blackened the gums and made the teeth look even whiter. Luckily it has gone out of fashion or we would have women with really scary vampire smiles!

Women wore a lot of jewellery—earrings, bangles, necklaces, bracelets for the wrists and upper arms, nose rings, hair ornaments, anklets and toe rings in many designs. The men were not far behind. Hindu women learnt to wear nose rings from Muslim women, and soon there was a wide variety of designs in vogue.

HAVING FUN

Music and dance were the main source of entertainment, and the famous singer Tansen found patronage in Akbar's court. The rich played polo, had fencing contests, horse races, archery, wrestling, boxing, a primitive form of hockey, and the kings watched elephant fights. Akbar was so passionate about polo, called chaugan, that he invented a bamboo ball with a piece of cloth soaked in oil placed inside that was lit, so that they could even play at night.

The pack of playing cards used by the Mughals had 144 cards of twelve suites each. One suite had a king, his vazir and ten soldiers, no queens or jacks. Chess continued to be popular and there were other board games like pachisi and chaupar. Books mention games called mughal pathan, lam turki and bhag chaal, but as the rules are not provided, it is difficult to understand how they were played.

WHOA! 'RAAG DEEPAK' DOESN'T LIGHT UP ONLY 'DEEPAKS'!!

WAH! WAH!

Through the year there were fairs and festivals, celebrated with
joyous abandon. The royal family also celebrated the Persian
New Year called Navroze. There were dance, music and folk
plays like Ramleela and travelling nautanki theatre groups.
Fairs would spring up regularly, and the largest religious fair
was the Kumbh Mela. The weekly markets called haats travelled
from village to village where the people did their shopping
and enjoyed watching animal races, acrobats, magicians and
jugglers. Poets recited their creations at mushairas, and singers
and dancers performed on makeshift stages.

Four: BRITISH INDIA

The People of British India

The Rulers of British India

THE PEOPLE OF BRITISH INDIA
(1800 CE–1940 CE)

A DAY IN THE LIFE OF MINI

Mini was going to school, and the house was in an uproar. Her grandmother said that if girls went to school, Lord Vishnu would get angry. Mokshada, the maid, was weeping because once Mini learnt to read and write, no one would marry her. It really puzzled Mini, why was Lord Vishnu against seven-year-old girls going to school? If her brother could do so, why couldn't she? She sighed. All she wanted to do was write her name—Kumari Mrinalini Mukhopadhya—on top of her exercise book.

'I'm sure Lord Vishnu would understand. Won't he, Baba?' she asked her father.

'Yes he will,' her father smiled down at her anxious face. 'Tell me something, who is the god of books?'

'A *goddess . . .*' Mini corrected him, 'the goddess Saraswati of course!'

'So if the goddess of books, knowledge and wisdom is a woman, how can Lord Vishnu mind a little girl going to school?'

'Very true,' Mini nodded and then added with a fierce frown, 'and if he does, I'll ask goddess Durga to do something about it.'

'Oh, absolutely! Durga would fix anyone who objects to girls going to school.'

'Oh, she will,' said Mini with satisfaction, and then picked up her shiny new school bag all packed with new books.

In the 18th century, as the Mughal Empire began to slowly fade away, new powers rose in the country and many of them were not Indian in origin. The Europeans—Portuguese, French, Dutch and English—came as traders and the Mughals allowed them to set up trading posts at ports like Surat and Cochin. One day they would build towns like Calcutta, Madras and Pondicherry, have their own private armies, and fight both Indian kings and each other. By the end of the 18th century, the English had triumphed over the other European powers. India became their largest colony, the 'jewel in the crown' of the British monarchy.

The British ruled over India for two centuries. First it was the East India Company that ruined Indian economy and made its officers so rich they were called 'nabobs'. Then after the Uprising of 1857, the British government took over the running of their richest colony. So we had Englishmen arriving at India's shores as army officers, administrators of the Indian Civil Services, businessmen and missionaries. Indians were introduced to a new religion—Christianity—a new language—English—and to European culture. What is interesting is that not just the Indians, but also the English, were changed by this encounter. And we get a portrait of British India through a wealth of not just histories, memoirs and government reports, but also photographs, paintings, gossipy diaries and recipe books.

The 18th century was a time of great turmoil as the Europeans, Marathas and the Mughals battled for the ownership of the land. So when the British finally triumphed the people were quite relieved, as now there would be peace at least. In many ways daily life in the cities and villages went on pretty much as before, but the attitudes of the people gradually changed through their interactions with the Europeans and the work of social reformers and the government.

The biggest changes that happened were the introduction of modern education in English instead of Sanskrit or Persian. Social reforms began with the emancipation of women and also a growing opposition to the caste system and the power of Brahmin priests. Finally, there was the introduction of technology—railways, the post and telegraph system, modern factories and machines—that transformed people's lives. India began to change, and with it did the daily lives of the people.

LIVING BY RULES

The life of the people was ruled by religion and superstitious beliefs. The Brahmin priest or the Maulvi dominated their daily lives because they were often the only literate men around, especially in villages. So they could control people through their readings of the sacred texts and astrological charts. They dictated how people lived, how they married, celebrated festivals and even what they ate. Hindus were afraid of losing their caste and blindly obeyed what the priest said. So their lives were full of absurd and expensive religious rituals. For example, the Hindu almanacs would tell you what fruits and vegetables were to be eaten on what day. Imagine losing your caste because you ate a banana on a Tuesday!

The life of ordinary people remained very difficult. Farmers were extremely poor as all the profit was made by the zamindars who taxed them ruthlessly. Famines happened frequently, and neither the government nor the zamindars did much to help.

WHAT?? YOU ATE A BANANA ON A TUESDAY AND NOW WANT ME TO FIND A SOLUTION?

During Mughal times, one of our biggest industries was textile weaving, and many in villages were weavers. Then as the British started selling cheap factory-made cottons, the weavers lost work and were forced to migrate to cities where they lived in horrific slums and worked as daily wage labourers.

The rich in the cities, usually traders, moneylenders and zamindars, lived in luxurious mansions, served by an army of servants, and squeezed every paisa out of the poor. These men made their money by working with the English; for them their colonial masters were like gods. So they spent their time worshipping their angrez deities, who lived in palatial mansions in Bombay, Madras and along Calcutta's famous road called Chowringhee, enjoying parties and dances, and riding around in luxurious carriages. As a matter of fact, the few men who did care for the poor were the British administrators—the district collectors, judges, police and army officers, who often showed them greater kindness than rich Indians.

Then there was the disgraceful caste system that divided Hindu society. The worst fate was reserved for the lowest castes considered untouchables. As a matter of fact, Dalits gained from a colonial government as they were offered both education and work but Hindu society did not make it easy. For example, B.R. Ambedkar's father was in the army and he educated all his sons. A brilliant student, Ambedkar studied in Britain and the United States and when he came back to India, the Maharaja of Baroda offered him a job. However, he was forced to decline the offer because no one would rent a room to him in Baroda and his colleagues refused to share a meal with him.

A TRAIN REVOLUTION

We take trains for granted, but in the 19th century these chugging machines puffing out smoke were like scary monsters

GUYS, IT'S ONLY A TRAIN!

for people who would run away every time a train went past! Then to their delight they discovered that these monsters travelled much faster than bullock carts, and soon every town wanted its own railway station. Of course, the British did not build the railways or start post and telegraphs for the benefit of the people. They needed to transport their goods and armies faster and cheaper and communicate between provinces in order to administer their colony. However, trains, the lowly postcard and telegrams completely changed the way people lived, travelled and kept in touch with each other.

In today's hyper connected world where we have a phone in our pocket and an email travels in seconds, it is hard to imagine how isolated people's lives were even a hundred and fifty year ago. Most people never left their villages or towns in their lives! One reason was that superstitious Brahmins told them they would lose their caste if they travelled. And if you crossed the seas, then of course the sky would fall and the world would come to an end! So for a person living in Lucknow, a city like Madras was on another planet, and you could live a lifetime without meeting anyone who spoke in a different language.

The first railway line opened in 1853 between Bombay and Thane, and soon a shiny network of steel was laid across the Indian landscape. The railways transformed lives in unexpected ways. As people sat together on the wooden benches of crowded compartments sharing samosas and tea in earthen cups, they discovered they had much in common. They shared traditions of religion, festivals, food and clothes. Then as factories came up across the country, the more enterprising men went to distant places to work. On the factory floor, a Bihari and a Keralite worked together and talked to each other in English. Then their families arrived and the children played together. In this quiet, unplanned way, we began to feel like a nation.

Trains made Indians lose their fear of travelling as they discovered that their world did not collapse when they left their villages. Even the intolerant bonds of caste loosened a little because when you work or travel together, it is not possible to make distinctions among castes. Earlier people derived their identity from their family name, caste and the village they lived in. Now it led to a gradual sense of being from the same country and of being Indians. This feeling of belonging to the same nation became an important factor during our freedom movement when we did not fight for a Tamil homeland or an Assamese nation: we fought for India. And curiously, it all begins with trains!

THE DARK AGES

Few boys went to school and no girls ever did, so the state of education was appalling. In 1911, out of a hundred men only eleven could read and write, and out of a hundred women only one was literate. This meant that the few educated men, usually priests, moneylenders, landowners and traders, controlled the lives of the others. Children had almost no childhood as boys were put to work early, and the girls were married off at the age of eight or ten to spend their lives inside their homes, doing housework and bringing up children.

For boys, going to school was no fun at all. Classes were held by priests who taught such yawningly boring subjects as religious texts, a bit of mathematics and utterly useless ones like logic and rhetoric. In higher classes, you could study astrology but not astronomy, mantras and talismans but not modern medicine. No one had heard of physics, chemistry, biology or even geography! Most of these amateur teachers were not that well educated and just taught by rote. They would yell and hit the poor students, so it is hardly surprising that most of them soon stopped attending school.

Just like building the rail network, the introduction of the English language and of a modern curriculum was done for a purely imperial reason, and once again the results were a real surprise. It all began with a rather superior Englishman, who thought Indians were backward and uncivilized and needed to be saved—Thomas Babington Macaulay. He decided that the 'natives' could be improved by European culture and English education. Hence he wrote a proposal to the government saying that all the work in offices, law courts, police and army should be in English instead of Persian, and that Indians should therefore be taught in that language. The government liked the idea because then they could have Indian clerks doing all the boring work at low wages, and these men would also be loyal to the government.

British missionaries were the first to open schools in India and boys keen to get jobs in the government poured in through their doors. The brighter ones then went off to colleges to study law, medicine, science and engineering and were soon part of a new middle class. Initially these men were exactly what Macaulay wanted—blindly loyal to the British and being 'brown sahibs', they would reject everything Indian. There are many stories about these haughty Indian babus who only wore suits and ties; spoke in English at home and had porridge and toast for breakfast.

With the arrival of printing presses, books were produced cheaply and textbooks were translated into regional languages. The first English school opened in Calcutta in 1800 and the first college, the Hindu College, was set up in 1871, where teachers like Henry Derozio encouraged students to question everything.

These rebellious young men quite enjoyed shocking society by their trendy western ways. One angry father wrote in a Calcutta newspaper that his son refused to wear Indian clothes, would not follow any religious rituals and had gone to the Kalighat temple and greeted the image of goddess Kali with a casual, 'Good morning, Madam!' Priests declared in ringing tones that Hindu society cursed by the gods would collapse because young men smoked cigars and little girls went to school. However, to their utter disappointment, nothing catastrophic happened!

This attitude of loyalty changed as Indians learnt about the French and American revolutions, and the concept of democracy. They all sat up and asked a very important question—What gives the British the right to rule over us? And then followed the great rallying cry—we want freedom! This would lead to a group of lawyers, teachers and social activists starting a political party in 1885 called the Indian National Congress. These men and women would lead the country not just to independence but also reform society. Surprisingly, Macaulay had anticipated this and had written in his famous 'Minute on Indian Education' in 1835, 'Come what may, self-knowledge will lead to self-rule and that would be the proudest day in British history.'

IN THE FAMILY

Education opens the mind as one learns to judge and ask questions. Modern education thus started huge changes in homes. One of the first questions these educated young men asked was—what was wrong with India? If a small European country could come and conquer India then there was something very wrong with our society. The brightest among them soon realized what we needed was modern education, an end to religious superstitions, a shift away from blind faith in the priesthood and finally the emancipation of women.

Raja Rammohan Roy started the Brahmo Samaj, going back to a pure form of Hinduism without rituals. At the Samaj prayers, members recited Sanskrit shlokas, and ceremonies like weddings were held without priests or expensive rituals. The members of the Samaj opened schools for girls and soon women were defying the purdah and stepping out of their homes. Ishwar Chandra Vidyasagar fought against the horrible practice of sati, opposed child marriages and then led a movement in support of the marriage of widows.

There were absurd objections as conservative men declared that educated girls were disobedient, and a superstitious belief was prevalent that the husbands of educated girls died young and so they became widows very quickly! Then as the first batch of female graduates passed out of Calcutta University in the 1890s, a remarkable young woman named Kadambini Basu became the first lady doctor in India. She went to Edinburgh to study medicine and came back to practise in Calcutta, travelling alone around the city in a phaeton carriage. More women chose a public life during the freedom movement, when answering the call of Mahatma Gandhi they stepped out to march proudly into the big, wide world.

THE CHILLI ARRIVES!

The arrival of the Europeans changed many of our food habits and the biggest contributions came, oddly enough, from the Portuguese. If you read the recipe books of the Mughals, you'll notice that they only used pepper to make a dish pungent, not chilli powder. Also, they used tamarind or curd to add sourness to their cooking, not tomatoes. That is because the green chilli and the tomato that we always have in our kitchens today are not natives of India!

The Portuguese had colonies in Mexico and South America and they introduced fruits and vegetables grown by the Mayans

of Mexico and the Incas of Peru. Here's an astonishing list of produce that only arrived in India after the 18th century—corn, potato, tomato, sweet potato, tapioca, peanuts, capsicum, papaya, pineapple and cashew nuts from the New World of North and South America. Also, coffee from Arabia, tea and soya beans from China. So Akbar never relished tomato chutney and Shivaji did not enjoy a plate of potato bhajis with a refreshing cup of tea!

The Europeans, and especially the British, may be blamed for the many ills of colonialism, but they did drag Indian society into the modern world. Today's Internet and Facebook generation knows that nothing transforms a society as effectively as education and good communication. You can't keep us in the dark ages if we can read, write, travel and talk to each other. With trains, postcards, telegrams, factories, schools, colleges, the English language and printing presses, our society became much more open and progressive and we became united as Indians. To be fair, we have to thank the British Empire for that.

THE RULERS OF BRITISH INDIA
(1800 CE–1940 CE)

A DAY IN THE LIFE OF ADIL

Adil watched carefully as his father laid the table, the way he folded a frilled napkin, placed the forks and knives and polished the wine glasses. His father was the khansama of Baker Sahib, who was the Collector Sahib of Sitapur.

Soon the guests would arrive for dinner, the women in long gowns and gloves, and the men in suits and cravats. Then as they sat down at the dining table, Adil and his father would bring in soups in the china bowls, plates of roast beef, mutton curry and pulao. After this, only his father would pour the wine as Adil was not allowed to touch those fragile crystal decanters.

'Abbu,' he asked his father, 'do you think I'll make a good khansama one day?'

His father held up a wine glass and squinted, 'I can see the marks of your fingers on this glass. No khansama would allow that.'

'Why do they need so many glasses anyway?' Adil wondered. 'And forks, spoons, knives . . .'

'Who knows!' his father sighed. 'I still get confused sometimes: soup spoons, dessert spoons, bread knife, meat knife . . .'

'I like the Mughals,' Adil said thoughtfully, 'they never used knives or forks. And instead of these tasteless roasts and soggy puddings, they ate pulaos and kebabs, paranthas and phirni. If they ever came back I'd apply for a job.'

'You do that, but now bring the cutlery box.'

◆ ◆ ◆

After the Uprising of 1857, the East India Company was disbanded and the British Government officially took over the colony of India. By a solemn proclamation, Queen Victoria became the new Empress of India and called upon her subjects 'to be faithful and bear true allegiance' to her.

There was just one problem with getting a new empress: India already had hundreds of rulers all claiming royal descent and divine authority to rule. They were maharajas, rajas, nawabs, sardars, thakurs, rawals and one unique Nizam—562 kingdoms, big, small and tiny, scattered across the Indian subcontinent. The solution was that the British ruled over the areas they controlled, which was about three-fifths of the country, and let the Indian kings continue to rule in what they called the 'Indian Principalities'. The kingdoms ranged from huge, prosperous ones like Kashmir, Hyderabad, Mysore, Travancore, Jaipur and Patiala to tiny dots on the map like Tonk, Limbdi and Sangli.

It must have been really tough to draw a map of India as it looked like a patchwork blanket with large areas of one colour, usually pink, and in between splashes of every colour in the palette. These bits were the many-hued and extravagant kingdoms, some as large as the Nizam's kingdom of Hyderabad

and Berar that covered 82,700 square miles. In fact in the 1930s, this kingdom had an annual income of nine crore rupees. At the other end of the scale was the kingdom of Vejanoness in Western India, where the thakur ruled over twenty-two acres and had the magnificent annual income of 450 rupees. His royal highness did not get a gun salute, but he was a king too!

YOUR ROYAL HIGHNESS

For all their pomp and pageantry, the Indian kings were not really independent rulers. They survived only because the British allowed them to do so, and almost all of them had to acknowledge that they were servants of the British Crown. There really was just one true ruler of India, and she was an empress that the poor villager called, 'Hamari Maharani Bictoria'.

The Indian kings had very little power. They had to pay for battalions of the British army that were stationed in their kingdoms, and there was a Resident Sahib who watched all the happenings at the royal court and interfered in everything. So just to hold on to their thrones, they kept busy trying to please their new masters and neglected the welfare of their subjects.

What was important to these powerless puppets were irrelevant things like the gun salute. Queen Victoria got a 101 gun salute, the Viceroy got thirty-one and below came 118 'salute states' squabbling over twenty-one to nine salutes. At all formal gatherings, they arrived wearing gaudy brocaded clothes, dripping with jewellery and carrying huge swords as if they were about to ride out to war! At home they led lives of idle luxury and of such flashy extravagance that even today books are being written about the extraordinary lives of Indian princes.

They had numerous palaces and huge harems. One Nizam had four official queens, forty-two begums and forty-four

MAHARAJ, WE HAVE RUN OUT OF AMMUNITION, SO NO GUN SALUTES TODAY!!

khannazads or 'palace women'. A maharaja of Patiala built a separate palace for his fifty or so children and their nannies and tutors. And a nawab of Rampur employed ninety chefs, who just cooked one dish a day!

What was it like to be born into an Indian royal family in the 19th century? The parents of the princes and princesses were always trying to copy the British royal family, so the children led an odd mix of traditional Indian and European lifestyles. They had English governesses and nannies, learnt nursery rhymes and had horses to ride. The boys were sent off to study at renowned schools like Eton, and then came back to traditional arranged marriages with dowries, wedding processions with elephants, and dancing nautch girls.

When the Mayo College was opened at Ajmer exclusively for princes, Jay Singh of Alwar arrived on an elephant accompanied by a big entourage of servants. Life was all about playing polo, banquets, durbars and tiger shoots. Once these princes sat on the throne, all their European education dissipated and they became autocratic rulers who gave no importance to words like democracy or human rights.

Europe was fascinated by the rajas and their wild, medieval ways. So gossip magazines carried scandalous tales about them, describing how they lived in huge palaces furnished with silk carpets and chandeliers, employed thousands of servants, dined off gold plates and had garages filled with Rolls Royce cars. On trips to Europe the exotic queens broke their purdah and stepped out at parties at the Ritz, shopped at Harrods and Cartier, and gambled at casinos. One maharani had a diamond necklace that had belonged to Josephine, the wife of Napoleon. A maharaja had a seven-string necklace made of pearls the size of pigeon's eggs. The dog-loving Nawab of Junagadh spent a fortune holding canine weddings, and a particular Nizam turned a Rolls Royce car into a garbage dump just because he felt the car salesman had been rude to him!

It was all very exciting, and everyone forgot about the poor and exploited subjects of these kingdoms. The people in British India at least got an efficient administration, modern education, medical care, technology like roads and railways, but most of the kingdoms ruled by autocratic kings still lived in a feudal age. Mahatma Gandhi felt that the Indian princes were 'perhaps the greatest blot on British rule in India'.

A few enlightened kings like Sayajirao Gaekwad of Baroda did set up schools and colleges, was a patron of classical music and gave scholarships for studying abroad. He fought against untouchability, and one student he selected was the extraordinary B.R. Ambedkar, who would fight for the rights of Dalits and lead the Constituent Assembly in drafting the Indian Constitution. Another remarkable ruler was a smart, independent woman—Begum Sultan Jahan of Bhopal—who was surprisingly modern in her outlook. Even though she appeared in a veil publicly, she ran an efficient administration and opened schools for girls. So in Princely India it all depended on luck: if you were fortunate, you got a good ruler.

Among all these sycophantic princes, the only ruler who showed a touch of independence was Maharana Fateh Singh of Udaipur, a proud descendent of Rana Pratap. He did not bow before George V at the Dilli Durbar of 1911, just like his Sisodia clan's earlier king Rana Pratap had never bowed before the Mughal king Akbar. Maharana Fateh Singh had been persuaded to come to Delhi for the durbar but then after watching the other kings he got so disgusted, that he refused to join the celebrations and went back home. Today, the Udaipur museum proudly displays the chair in which he *never* sat in Delhi.

SAHIBS AND MEMS

The presence of the English in towns and cities influenced the life of Indians in many ways. At the same time the English were also changed by their stay in a strange, hot country where no one had heard of Yorkshire pudding or Trafalgar Square.

Indians taught them a horse game called chaugan that they renamed polo, and they taught Indians cricket and football. Their greatest gift, however, was the English language that opened the world of European science and literature to Indians and soon became the lingua franca of the country. The spices of India transformed the insipid English menu, and today words like curry and dosa can be found in the pages of the Oxford Dictionary. However, we definitely did not teach them to make a weird hybrid dish called Chicken Tikka Masala; that is a pure British creation.

India has been conquered many a time before, but there is one big difference between, say, the Mughals and the British. The earlier invaders came to stay and gradually merged with the people; the British never really made India their home. Very consciously they led completely separate lives, with homes within gated cantonments, and only socialized with each other. Except for a few English families like the Trevors, Rivet-Carnacs and Ogilvys who made India their home for generations, once the men retired from service, most of the families went back to Britain.

As one reads the many nostalgic memoirs written by old India hands, what comes through is how little they really learnt about the daily lives of the people who lived in the narrow lanes and teeming bazaars outside their bungalows. The men knew the Indians they met at work; the women mention the servants, and the children tell fond stories of ayahs and malis. They never mention childhood friends who were Indians. Indian society, too, chose to keep them out of their homes. Hindus had superstitions about caste and pollution, the Muslims had women in purdah and, most importantly, there was the barrier of language which came in the way of forging ties.

The first Englishmen who came as traders, the 'nabobs' of the 18th century, had a more easygoing attitude and mixed freely with Indians. They learnt the local language, lived like Indian nobility, wore comfortable kurta-pyjamas, smoked hookahs and chewed paan. They enjoyed watching nautch girls and some even married Indian women. But by Victorian times this attitude had hardened as men came with families, and the disapproving memsahibs put a stop to all the nautch nonsense. Now there was a sense of superiority and at times downright contempt for everything Indian. In small towns across India, the lives of the Englishmen were limited to work, home, tennis at the club and double whiskies at the army mess.

The English found the Indian climate hard to bear and often shifted to the hills in summer. This was how hill stations like Simla, Darjeeling, Mussoorie, Ootacamund and Murree were developed. Here they tried to create a replica of English life with red tiled roof bungalows, theatres, shopping arcades and racing tracks. The cottages had names like 'Rose Villa' and 'Hill View', and the English spent their times going to balls and the theatre where the only brown skin among the guests would be an occasional maharaja. The government used to shift to Simla in summer and so did the Indian staff, but the Indian families stayed in carefully separated localities down the hill. Many Indians worked all their lives in the government but never saw the inside of an English home.

The segregation was quite open and without apology. In Simla, Indians were not allowed to shop in the Mall because according to the Municipality rules, they were 'ill dressed', that is they wore saris and dhotis. There were separate schools and hospitals for the English, on trains there were carriages marked 'For Europeans Only', and they even had compartments reserved for the mixed race of Anglo-Indians. The two worlds of the 'mai baap' ruler and the 'koi hai' subjects were kept firmly separate.

SARIS AND DHOTIS NOT ALLOWED.

HINGLISH

We know that English words like 'sahib', 'bazaar' or 'shawl' came from Indian words. Here's a list of others you may never have thought of!

From Hindi—brinjal (baingan), bungalow (bangla), camphor (kapur), juggernaut (Jagannath), kedgeree (khichri), sepoy (sipahi), shampoo (champi), sherbet (sarbat)

From Sanskrit—cash (karsha), pepper (pippali), sugar (sarkara)

From Tamil—candy (kandi), coir (kayiru), mango (mankay)

From Malayalam—betel (vettila), ginger (inchiver)

And the word tamarind comes from the Arabic phrase—'tamur-ul-Hindi', meaning the date of India!

THE BABA LOG

The memories of British children who grew up in India are all about the sights, smells and colours of the land, not about playing hopscotch with a Hindu friend. No one talks about Indian families being invited to lunch or shopping with a woman in a sari. What they missed in England, as one writer Jennifer Brennan says, was 'the stealthy waft of incense from the temple' and the 'burst of fresh dampness as the first monsoon raindrops hit the parched earth'. And they never forgot the tropical colours, the 'vivid clashes of magenta, yellow, scarlet and pink of the zinnias echoing the swaying saris in the crowded streets of the Old Quarter.' It's as if they had gone on an extended holiday to an exotic, mysterious land.

India's climate was not easy on the children and many succumbed to diseases like cholera and malaria. Old cemeteries across the country are filled with these heartbreakingly tiny gravestones. After being spoilt by their ayahs, they were often separated from their families and sent off to study in harsh English boarding schools. Many, like the writer Spike Milligan, dreamed of going back to India as he found 'England was a gloomy, dull, grey land.'

Life was very easy in India with an army of servants, and one book lists thirty-six types of servants employed by an average household. There were the usual khansama (head bearer), mali (gardener), bawarchi (cook), ayah (maid) and dhobi (washerman). Also odd ones like harkara (messenger), who was somehow different from a peon, hajjam (barber), farash (furniture keeper), syce (stable hand) and duria (dog keeper). So the memsahib really had nothing to do all day except give instructions, arrange flowers and then plan what to wear to the club in the evening.

The sahibs were exposed more to the real India and many of them had a kind but superior attitude towards Indians. For them Indians were like children who had to be cared for and

GOOD MORNING CHAPS!
IT'S SO HOT TODAY!

also disciplined. Some officials were arrogant and cruel, it is true, but many more had a genuine interest in helping people. These men of the Indian Civil Service, in their khakis and sola topi, perched on charpais in village chaupals and listened to the peasants. They were much more honest and helpful compared to the earlier Mughal officials. As a matter of fact once the British left, these men were missed the most by the poor people of the country.

Many of the sahibs added a touch of amusing eccentricity to Indian life. There was the Collector Sahib who drove to the club in the evening in a horse drawn barouche while his grim-faced wife followed him on a bicycle. Another decided on a new weather-friendly summer wardrobe and would bicycle to office in khaki shorts, a sleeveless cotton vest and his comfy 'chapplis', shocking his superiors who would be sweating away in their dark, heavy suits.

MULLIGATAWNY MA'AM!

The English came to India in search of spices and soon cloves, cardamom, pepper and coriander changed their cuisine. It began with all the bawarchis in their kitchens adding an Indian touch to soups and roasts. Finding it hard to cook without spices and uncomfortable with baking, these bawarchis in their dark smoky cookhouses introduced their sahibs to the subtle flavours of pulaos and kormas, chutneys and pickles. Soon there was a blending of Indian and European cuisines that produced unique Anglo-Indian creations like kedgeree and Mulligatawny soup.

The memsahibs did try to teach the bawarchis their way of cooking, but somehow Indians never really took to it. Few Indians eat English dishes except for the breads, biscuits, cakes, jams and omelettes on their breakfast table and the perennial caramel custard on the menu of railway station restaurants.

It is doubtful that any self-respecting bawarchi would have created what the English call a 'curry' because no authentic Indian cuisine has a dish of that name, and neither do we have anything called curry powder.

Recipe books written by Burra Mems list some very odd dishes. There is of course the legendary kedgeree, always served at breakfast. It is based on the Indian khichri but while the Indian version is a simple mix of rice, lentil and spices, kedgeree is a rich dish made with flaked fish and hard boiled eggs! The Tamils drank a light vegetarian soup called 'mulago tanni' or pepper water, and this was transformed into the rich Mulligatawny soup with mutton and chicken. The English curry with a mysterious spice mix called 'curry powder' was made with meat, apples, raisins and dollops of cream, and it was not Indian at all.

They loved their Mulligatawny so much someone even wrote a ditty to it:

> In vain our hard-fate we repine;
> In vain our fortune we rail;
> On *Mullaghee-tawny* we dine,
> Or *Congee*, in Bangalore Jail.

The food habits of the English were very different and they did eat a lot. There was *chhota hazri* or bed tea, followed by *burra hazri* or breakfast when families sat down to a huge meal at eleven in the morning, a light *tiffin* or lunch and dinner around six in the evening. One book lists a typical breakfast with mutton chops, chicken cutlets, devilled kidneys, various kinds of egg dishes, duck stews, prawn do-piaza, a platter of breads and of course kedgeree. The regular dinner menu, according to Eliza Fay writing in 1800, was 'a soup, a roast fowl, curry and rice, a mutton pie, a forequarter of lamb, a rice pudding, tarts, very good cheese, fresh churned butter, fine breads and excellent Madeira.'

The recipe books have some very strange names of Anglo-Indian dishes in an impossible contortion of Indian words. Take a look at 'kulleah bungooday': maybe kulleah is our kalia but what on earth is a bungooday? There was pish-pash, dhobie pie (how many dhobis do you know who eat pies?), many variations of something called foogath and finally the pièce de résistance—Qui Hai Salad Dressing!

MORE HISTORY HUNGAMA

MORE HISTORY
HUNGAMA

WHAT HAPPENED AND WHEN

BCE (Before the Common Era)

- 3000–1500: Harappan civilization
- 1500–1200: Age of the Rig Veda
- 600: Rise of kingdoms and republics like Magadha, Kosala and Vaishali
- 560–467: Life of Vardhaman Mahavira, Jain Tirthankara
- 556–468: Life of Siddhartha Gautama, the Buddha
- 362–321: Nanda dynasty ruling Magadha
- 326–325: Invasion of Alexander of Macedon
- 321: Chandragupta Maurya becomes king of Magadha
- 268–231: Rule of Ashoka of the Mauryan dynasty

CE (Common Era)

- 78: Kanishka of the Kushan dynasty becomes king
- 300–500: the Gupta Empire
- 319–335: Rule of Chandragupta I
- 335–375: Rule of Samudragupta
- 375–415: Rule of Chandragupta II Vikramaditya
- 500: Rise of the Pallavas in the south
- 606–647: Rule of Harshavardhana of Kanauj
- 899–1300: Rise of the Chola dynasty in the south
- 1001–1027: Invasions of Mahmud of Ghazni
- 1192: Prithviraj Chauhan defeated by Muhammad of Ghur
- 1206: Beginning of the Sultanate of Delhi
- 1320–1388: Rule of the Tughlak dynasty of Delhi
- 1336–1565: Vijayanagar Empire in the south

- 1398: Timur the Mongol conqueror invades India
- 1498: Vasco da Gama arrives at the Indian coast
- 1526: Babur defeats Ibrahim Lodi at the First Battle of Panipat
- 1526–1530: Rule of Babur, founder of the Mughal Empire
- 1556–1605: Rule of the Mughal emperor Akbar
- 1605–1627: Rule of Jahangir and Nurjahan
- 1615: The East India Company begins trade in India
- 1628–1657: Rule of Shahjahan
- 1630–1680: Life of the Maratha king, Shivaji
- 1658–1707: Rule of Aurangzeb
- 1690: City of Calcutta founded by the English
- 1739: Nadir Shah of Persia ransacks Delhi
- 1757: Battle of Plassey. Robert Clive defeats Sirajuddaulah, Nawab of Bengal
- 1761: Third Battle of Panipat, Ahmad Shah Abdali defeats the Marathas
- 1764: Battle of Buxar. East India Company acquires the diwani of Bengal
- 1829: Prohibition of sati
- 1835: English declared the official language of the government
- 1853: First railway and telegraph lines
- 1857–1858: Uprising against the English led by the sepoys of the army
- 1877: Queen Victoria proclaimed the Empress of India
- 1885: Foundation of the Indian National Congress
- 1905: Partition of Bengal leads to widespread protests
- 1906: Foundation of the All India Muslim League
- 1909: The Minto-Morley Act gives Muslims separate electorates
- 1911: Delhi Durbar with George V. Delhi, the new capital of the British Empire
- 1919: Massacre at Jallianwalla Bagh, Amritsar
- 1920–1922: Non-Cooperation Movement led by Mahatma Gandhi
- 1921: Montagu-Chelmsford Act
- 1928: Congress resolution for Purna Swaraj, complete independence
- 1930: Mahatma Gandhi leads the Dandi March to protest the Salt Tax
- 1937: Elections in eleven provinces, Congress ministries in eight
- 1942: Quit India movement
- 1947: Partition of the country into Pakistan and India
- 15 August 1947: India becomes an independent nation.

THINGS TO DO WITH HISTORY

History books can be really scary, big, fat and full of long paragraphs. Another problem with Indian history is that there is just so much: five thousand years of it! And we are supposed to remember all that!

I do understand that you get sort of nervous about finding out more of India's history. Here are a few ways to get to the interesting bits and discover all the fascinating things about our past without yawning!

And if you have a weird question or need a quick history check, you can email me at subhadrasg@gmail.com. I promise to help.

Books to Read

I am not asking you to read all these books, honest! But if you are looking for information on Indian history, these books have it. Just look up the topic in the index at the back and zip to the page where you'll find it.

1. *India, a History*—John Keay. HarperCollins.
2. *An Advanced History of India*—Majumdar, Raychaudhuri and Datta. Macmillan.
3. *A History of South India*—K.A. Nilakanta Sastri. Oxford University Press.
4. *Daily Life in Ancient India*—Jeannine Auboyer. Munshiram Manoharlal.
5. *Ancient Indian Costumes*—Roshen Alkazi. Art Heritage.
6. *The First Spring: The Golden Age of India*—Abraham Eraly. Penguin.
7. *The Last Spring: The Great Mughals*—Abraham Eraly.
8. *The Discovery of India*—Jawaharlal Nehru. Oxford University Press.

9. *Indian Food, a Historical Companion*—K.T. Achaya. Oxford University Press.
10. *The Wonder That Was India*—A.L. Basham. Rupa.

Find History on the Internet

There is a lot of information on the Internet, though it is not always correct. So be careful. The miracle when looking for quick results is of course Google. Go to www.google.com and then just type the subject you are looking for. One website that is usually quite reliable is www.wikipedia.org.

Long Walks and Museum Visits

History really comes alive if you visit a monument. And old buildings are everywhere. You can touch the carvings on the wall in a temple or walk about a palace where a famous king once lived.

Then you can visit a museum and see the pots and pans, the clothes, jewellery and shoes and even the swords and guns used by people in the past. Most museums are *huuuge*, so don't even try to see everything. Pick the period you are interested in and visit that gallery. My favourites at the National Museum in Delhi are the gallery on Harappa and the one on Arms and Armour.

WHAT DID THEY SAY ABOUT US?

Travellers to India found our country pretty amazing, but also very puzzling. Their writings give us an idea of the life of the people in the past. So here are some quotations that will amuse you.

A. DEARE (1809)

'The higher classes of these men wear their beards long, and bushy up to the eyes, and are extremely fanciful in the colour of them, sometimes tingeing them with lilac, pink, light blue, yellow and even scarlet. I saw one man whose beard was white, edged with purple.'

MARK TWAIN (1898)

'So far as I am able to judge, nothing has been left undone, either by man or Nature, to make India the most extraordinary country that the sun visits on his round ... Always, when you think you have come to the end of her tremendous specialities and have finished hanging tags upon her as the Land of the Thug, the Land of the Plague, the Land of Famine, the Land of Giant Illusions, the Land of Stupendous Mountains and so forth, another speciality crops up and another tag is required. I have been overlooking the fact that India is by an unapproachable supremacy—the Land of Murderous Wild Creatures. Perhaps it will be simplest to throw away the tags and generalize her with one all-comprehensive name, the Land of Wonders.'

Mark Twain also discovered what he said was the longest title in the world. It was the title of a sadhu he met in India. Okay, here goes:

Sri 108 Matparamahansa-parivrajakacharya-swami-bhaskarananda-saraswati !!!

L.H. NIBLETT

L.H. NIBLETT wrote this poem after meeting an Indian astrologer:

THE INDIAN FORTUNE TELLER

He comes with mystic air, in flowing turmeric robes
With strings and strings of beads, with earrings on his lobes.
'I tell it Master's fortune,' he says in accents mild,
'You'll have it too much money and plenty wife and child.'
He speaks of great promotion, of lucky stars and bad
He tells me where I'll go and just when I'll be 'had'.
He gives the same old yarn, and tells me very soon,
I'll be a pompous General, on the 'thirty first' of June!

E.H. AITKEN (1889)

Aitken had a Goan cook named Domingo, whose English spellings and vocabulary were rather weak. This is a menu written by Domingo. Try to decipher it; I failed!

MENU
Soup—Salary Soup
Fis—Heel fish fry
Madish—Russel pups. Wormsil mole
Joint—Roast Bastard
Toast—Anchovy Poshteg
Puddin—Billimunj. Ispunj roli